CAMPAIGN 326

THE SOLOMONS 1943–44

The Struggle for New Georgia and Bougainville

MARK STILLE

ILLUSTRATED BY PETER DENNIS

Series Editor Marcus Cowper

OSPREY PUBLISHING
Bloomsbury Publishing Plc

Kemp House, Chawley Park, Cumnor Hill, Oxford OX2 9PH, UK
29 Earlsfort Terrace, Dublin 2, Ireland
1385 Broadway, 5th Floor, New York, NY 10018, USA
Email: info@ospreypublishing.com
www.ospreypublishing.com

OSPREY is a trademark of Osprey Publishing Ltd

First published in Great Britain in 2018

© Osprey Publishing Ltd, 2018

A catalog record for this book is available from the British Library.

Print ISBN: 978 1 4728 2447 9
eBook: 978 1 4728 2449 3
ePDF: 978 1 4728 2450 9
XML: 978 1 4728 2448 6

Maps by www.bounford.com
3D BEVs by The Black Spot
Index by Alan Rutter
Typeset by PDQ Digital Media Solutions, Bungay, UK
Printed and bound in India by Replika Press Private Ltd.

22 23 24 25 26   10 9 8 7 6 5 4 3

The Woodland Trust
Osprey Publishing supports the Woodland Trust, the UK's leading
woodland conservation charity.

www.ospreypublishing.com
To find out more about our authors and books visit our website. Here
you will find extracts, author interviews, details of forthcoming events
and the option to sign-up for our newsletter.

ARTIST'S NOTE

Readers may care to note that the original paintings from which the color
plates in this book were prepared are available for private sale. All
reproduction copyright whatsoever is retained by the publishers. All
enquiries should be addressed to:

Peter Dennis, Fieldhead, The Park, Mansfield, Notts, UK, NG18 2AT
Email: magie.h@ntlworld.com

The publishers regret that they can enter into no correspondence upon
this matter.

Key to military symbols

CONTENTS

The Central and Northern Solomons, June 30, 1943

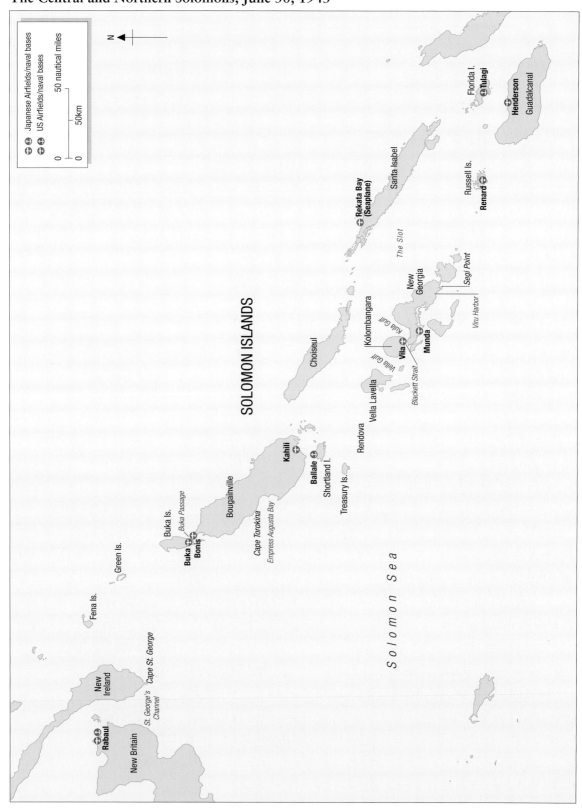

INTRODUCTION

The ultimate objective of the American campaign in the Solomon Islands was the neutralization or seizure of the major Japanese stronghold of Rabaul on the island of New Britain in the Bismarck Archipelago. The Japanese captured Rabaul in January 1942 and quickly turned it into their most important base in the South Pacific. Rabaul possessed a magnificent natural harbor and a complex of airfields. In the hands of the Japanese, it represented a potential springboard against the sea lines of communications (SLOC) between the United States and Australia, and potentially even against Australia itself. Defensively, Rabaul provided the Japanese with a solid position which blocked any Allied move against the Philippines and provided defensive depth to the Imperial Japanese Navy's (IJN) major Central Pacific base at Truk Atoll.

As early as July 1942, the Americans began to execute a plan to capture Rabaul. By this point, the threat of a major Japanese offensive deep into the South Pacific to cut Allied SLOCs by seizing the Fiji and Samoa Islands and the island of New Caledonia in the New Hebrides had been eliminated in the aftermath of major Allied victories at the Battle of the Coral Sea in May and Midway in June 1942. The American victory at Midway in particular had blunted the IJN's offensive power and forced the cancellation of planned attacks into the South Pacific, and enabled the Americans to put into place their plan to begin the advance against Rabaul.

The orders issued on July 2 by the US Joint Chiefs divided the campaign into three phases. The initial phase was to seize Tulagi and Guadalcanal Islands in the southern Solomons. The second phase called for the capture of the remainder of the Solomons and the northeastern part of New Guinea. The final phase was the capture of Rabaul itself.

Phase one proved difficult and lengthy. The Americans landed the 1st Marine Division on Tulagi and Guadalcanal on August 7. The landing brought an immediate response from the Japanese and a six-month grinding battle of attrition ensued. Tulagi was quickly captured, but Guadalcanal and its critical airfield became the scene of vicious fighting, both on land and at sea. The Americans did not possess any real measure of naval or air superiority over the Japanese at the start of the campaign. This, in combination with an uncertain logistical base, prolonged the campaign well past expectations. Both sides poured in more forces, but the Japanese were never able to seize the airfield or suppress it for any prolonged period, which meant that they could never move sufficient ground forces to the island. This meant the airfield stayed in American hands which gave them the advantage

Henderson Field on Guadalcanal, shown here in August 1942, was the focal point of the Guadalcanal campaign, which lasted six months. The airfields in the Central Solomons had the same importance, which meant that the next phase of the Solomons campaign was centered on Munda Airfield on New Georgia. (Naval History and Heritage Command)

and eventual victory. In the course of the campaign, six major naval actions were fought around the island with both sides suffering significant losses. Growing control of the air and sea around the island allowed the Americans to reinforce the garrison with another Marine division and two Army divisions. This force was able to expel the Japanese from the island in early February 1943.

By the end of the Guadalcanal campaign, the situation in the South Pacific had been significantly altered. The growing power of the US Navy was fully on display with a growing number of war-built ships reaching the Pacific. American airpower, which provided the difference in the campaign, was firmly in control of the airspace over the southern Solomons and beginning to execute raids against Japanese bases in the Central Solomons and even against Rabaul itself. In comparison, the IJN had suffered such severe losses that it felt compelled to disengage from the Guadalcanal campaign to save itself for a future decisive battle fought under better conditions. The IJN's air power, both carrier and land based, was also severely attrited and was never again the factor it had been earlier in the war. The Imperial Japanese Army (IJA) committed some 31,400 men to the island of which only 11,400 were evacuated. The Japanese ability to contest a renewed American advance into the central and northern Solomons had been severely degraded.

Concurrent with the fighting on Guadalcanal, there was another bitter campaign being waged on the Papuan Peninsula of New Guinea. Following the Japanese defeat in the Coral Sea, which thwarted their attempt to seize the Allied base of Port Moresby by sea, a small IJA force landed at Buna on the northeastern coast of the peninsula and tried to seize Port Moresby by a land attack. The attack lacked proper logistical support and was mounted over some of the most rugged terrain in the world. Not surprisingly, the attack faltered, and the Americans and Australians were able to deploy additional forces to secure the Papuan Peninsula. The campaigns in Papua and the Solomons were linked throughout 1942 and 1943. Rabaul was the primary Japanese support hub for both operations, and Japanese naval and air forces operating from Rabaul and other nearby bases had the ability to intervene in either area. The same IJA command supplied forces for both and was increasingly hard-pressed to do so, forcing the Japanese to make tough decisions about which campaign to support.

The drive on Rabaul was complicated from the Allied perspective by the fact that it was fought at the seam of the two major commands of the Pacific War. In March 1942, by agreement among the Allied nations operating in the area, as well as between the US Navy and the US Army which often had a difficult relationship, especially when it came to establishing which service had ultimate control over an area or operation, two large commands were set up to conduct the war in the Pacific. The area covering Australia, New Guinea, New Britain, and most of the Solomons was the responsibility of the Southwest Pacific Area. This was under the command of Army General Douglas MacArthur, who was based in Australia. The rest of the Pacific Theater was the purview of Admiral Chester W. Nimitz in his capacity as Commander in Chief of the Pacific Ocean Areas. Being so large, Nimitz's command was divided into three parts, the South, Central, and North Pacific Areas. The South Pacific Area included the SLOCs between the United States and Australia and the remainder of the Solomons. Nimitz did not exercise direct control of the South Pacific Area. Since October 1942, that was the responsibility of Vice Admiral William F. Halsey. Friction between the US Navy and the US Army was endemic throughout the war, but relations during the upcoming Solomons campaign were fairly good due to the mutual respect between Halsey and MacArthur.

The Solomons campaign was the first opportunity for the Americans to put into practice an island-hopping strategy. If successful, it had the potential to disrupt the Japanese defensive strategy of making the Americans fight for every island on the long road to Japan. The American campaign in the Solomons also featured 'triphibious' warfare in which air, ground, and naval forces had to be carefully synchronized—a prerequisite for a successful drive across the Pacific. The Japanese, having lost the initiative at Guadalcanal, were forced on the strategic defensive. While holding no illusions they could stop the American drive into the Solomons, they had every intention of delaying the Americans for as long as possible while inflicting the maximum number of casualties. The Solomons campaign was a fascinating case study of joint operations fought over some of the most difficult terrain in the world against a determined defender.

CHRONOLOGY

1943

April 7	Japanese open Operation *I* with a massive air raid on Allied shipping off Guadalcanal.
April 11–14	Japanese aircraft hit three locations on New Guinea after which Operation *I* is closed down; overall Allied losses are light.
April 18	Admiral Yamamoto, Commander of the Combined Fleet, is shot down over Bougainville and killed.
June 16	Last major daylight air strike over Guadalcanal results in heavy Japanese losses.
June 21	Marine Raiders seize Segi Point on New Georgia.
June 30	Americans land on Rendova Island against light opposition and repel three Japanese air raids.
June 30	Americans land at Wickham Anchorage and Viru on New Georgia.
July 2	Americans land at Zanana, about five miles from Munda Airfield on New Georgia.
July 4–8	The 43rd Division advances three miles toward Munda.
July 5	Northern Landing Force lands at Rice Anchorage on northwestern coast of New Georgia.
July 5	In an engagement in the Kula Gulf, one US Navy destroyer is sunk.
July 6	In the Battle of Kula Gulf, the IJN scores a tactical victory by sinking the light cruiser *Helena* while losing two destroyers.
July 9–15	The 43rd Division's attack to seize Munda is stopped.
July 13	The naval Battle of Kolombangara results in a Japanese victory with three Allied cruisers damaged and one destroyer sunk for the loss of a Japanese light cruiser.
July 14–17	The Japanese counterattack on New Georgia fails.
July 16–24	The Americans conduct only local attacks in the area of Munda.
July 18–20	The American attack to seize Bairoko, the Japanese supply terminus on New Georgia from Kolombangara, fails.
July 25	XIV Corps opens attack on Munda with two divisions supported by heavy air, artillery and naval gunfire support.
August 5	The Americans take Munda Airfield.
August 6	The Battle of Vella Gulf results in the first night engagement defeat for Japanese destroyers; three IJN destroyers are sunk.

August 15	The Americans land on Vella Lavella Island, northwest of New Georgia, to by-pass heavily defended Kolombangara.
August 18	Naval battle off Horaniu ends indecisively.
August 25	Bairoko falls.
September 28 –October 3	Japanese successfully evacuate most of the garrison on Kolombangara despite a US naval blockade.
October 6	The Battle of Vella Lavella ends indecisively; both sides lose a destroyer.
October 27	New Zealand troops land on Treasury Islands south of Bougainville.
November 1	3rd Marine Division lands at Cape Torokina on Bougainville to avoid heavily-defended southern Bougainville.
November 2	The Battle of Empress Augusta Bay, the largest naval encounter of the Solomons campaign, results in a decisive Japanese defeat; one IJN light cruiser and a destroyer are sunk.
November 7	Japanese counterlanding north of American beachhead is defeated.
November 21	American beachhead firmly established with two divisions ashore.
November 25	The Battle of Cape St. George results in a rout for the IJN; three Japanese destroyers are sunk for no US Navy losses.
December 24	American beachhead expands to maximum extent.

1944

March 9–17	A series of Japanese attacks on the American beachhead on Bougainville are repulsed with heavy Japanese losses.
March 23	Final Japanese attack on the beachhead fails.
Late December	Australian troops begin final drive to eliminate Japanese garrison on Bougainville.

1945

September 8	The Japanese garrison on Bougainville surrenders.

OPPOSING COMMANDERS

US COMMANDERS

Before operations could begin, the question of who would command the Solomons campaign had to be settled. The directive of July 2, 1942 which began the drive to Rabaul stated that phase two and three would be conducted under the command of MacArthur. This would place the bulk of the US Navy, then committed to the South Pacific, under Army control. This was simply unacceptable to the US Navy, so a compromise was arrived at. Halsey's forces, even though they were operating to the west of the 159-degree east longitude which marked the boundary between MacArthur's Southwest Pacific and Halsey's South Pacific commands, would remain under Navy and Halsey's control. The entire operation in the Solomons would be under MacArthur's 'general directives.'

General Douglas MacArthur in his capacity as Commander-in-Chief of the Southwest Pacific Area was in overall control of the operation. However, per the agreement outlined above, the actual conduct of the drive through the Solomons was under the command of **Vice Admiral William F. Halsey** in his capacity as Commander, South Pacific Force. MacArthur was famously difficult to get along with, and this was even more pronounced for Navy officers. However, MacArthur took a liking to Halsey, who had the reputation

Halsey had the benefit of some outstanding commanders on his South Pacific staff. This photo from September 1943 shows from left to right, Lt. Gen. Vandegrift, USMC, Adm. Halsey, Lt. Gen. Milliard Harmon, US Army, and Maj. Gen. Barrett, USMC. Harmon was highly regarded by Halsey and became his de facto deputy during the campaign. Barrett was the 3rd Marine Division's first commander before assuming command of I Marine Amphibious Corps (IMAC) on September 27 from Vandegrift. After Barrett's death on October 8, ruled an accident by the inquest looking into his death, but possibly a suicide after being relieved by Halsey, Vandegrift was recalled briefly to resume command of IMAC. After turning IMAC over to Geiger, Vandegrift went to Washington, DC to become the 18th Commandant of the Marine Corps. (Naval History and Heritage Command)

Rear Admiral Wilkinson planned the invasions of Vella Lavella and Bougainville. This photo from before the invasion of Leyte in October 1944 shows, left to right, Wilkinson, V. Adm. Thomas C. Kinkaid, Commander Seventh Fleet; and R. Adm. Daniel E. Barbey, Commander Amphibious Force, Seventh Fleet. (Naval History and Heritage Command)

as a fighting admiral, when they met for the first time on April 26, 1943. By this period of the war, Halsey was a legend following his early war carrier raids and his victory in the Guadalcanal campaign, where his aggression and determination to throw everything available into the fight turned the tide. Though he was criticized later in the war for condoning sloppy staff work and making poor decisions, by all accounts he was at the top of his game in 1943 and was able to turn his multinational and joint service staff into a smooth-functioning and effective command. He gave wide latitude to his air and ground commanders, but reserved the conduct of naval operations for himself. The naval portion of his command consisted of the Third Fleet, which was divided up into a number of subordinate task forces in the typical US Navy manner. The Amphibious Force was commanded by **Rear Admiral Richmond K. Turner**. He had commanded the amphibious forces during the Guadalcanal campaign and despite a reputation of being hard to work with, was to become the US Navy's premier practitioner of large-scale amphibious operations. In July, Turner went to the Central Pacific to serve under Nimitz, and he was relieved by **Rear Admiral Theodore S. Wilkinson**. Wilkinson is one of the lesser-known US Navy admirals of the war, but became a very proficient practitioner of amphibious warfare. He graduated top of his class at Annapolis in 1909 and had a gunnery background. At the start of the war he was the Director of Naval Intelligence before moving to the South Pacific in January 1943 and taking over III Amphibious Force in June 1943. He planned and conducted the invasions of Vella Lavella and Bougainville.

The naval forces covering operations in the Solomons were usually divided into two task groups. **Rear Admiral Walden L. Ainsworth** commanded one and **Rear Admiral A. Stanton Merrill** the other. US Navy destroyer commanders were ultra-aggressive during the campaign, led by then **Captain Arleigh A. Burke**. Burke was in command of Destroyer Squadron 23, which saw almost constant action during the campaign. He went on to be

Mitscher's chief of staff and after the war became Chief of Naval Operations. By this point in the war, the US Navy had weeded out all but the most aggressive officers. These officers learned from earlier American mistakes in the Guadalcanal campaign. They also proved willing and able to embrace and incorporate technology into their planning and tactics.

Overall command of Allied land-based aircraft in the Solomons was exercised by **Vice Admiral Aubrey W. Fitch**, Commander, South Pacific Air Forces. Fitch was an experienced airman who had commanded carriers earlier in the war. The command of Allied air forces in the Solomons was rotated to facilitate interservice cooperation. **Rear Admiral Marc A. Mitscher** took over in early April. Mitscher had a reputation as a fighter who was able to inspire his men. He performed so well in the Solomons that he was given command of the US Navy's Fast Carrier Task Force and played a central role in the drive to Tokyo during the final year and a half of the war. The 13th Air Force, the Army Air Force component of Allied air forces in the Solomons, was commanded by **Major-General Nathan F. Twining**. He assumed command of Allied air forces in the Solomons on July 25.

The commanding general of US Army troops in the South Pacific Area was **Lieutenant-General Milliard F. Harmon, Jr.** His principal duties were administrative, but he was also a key advisor to Halsey on operational issues and became a de facto deputy commander during the New Georgia campaign. **Major-General John H. Hester** was the commander of the 43rd Division and he was assigned command of the entire New Georgia Occupation Force. This proved too much for a divisional staff to handle, and later in the campaign **Major-General Oscar W. Griswold**, commander of XIV Corps, took over responsibility for operations. The commander of the 37th Division was **Major-General Robert S. Beightler**. He was a National Guard officer but was highly regarded, as was shown by the fact that he was the only National Guard officer to train his division before the war and then lead it for the duration of the conflict. **Major-General J. Lawton Collins** commanded the 25th Division. He had a proven combat record from Guadalcanal and would go on to fight in Europe with distinction.

For the Bougainville phase of the Solomons campaign, the US Marine Corps provided the landing force. These were under the command of **Lieutenant-General Alexander A. Vandegrift**, USMC, hero of the battle for Guadalcanal. Vandegrift had been selected to become Commandant of the Marine Corps, but was called to take temporary command of the ground

On June 16, 1943, Adm. Nimitz, Commander in Chief, Pacific, visited V. Adm. Fitch's headquarters on Espiritu Santo, New Hebrides. Present are, from left to right: Maj. Gen. Ralph H. Mitchell, USMC (Commander Marine Aircraft, South Pacific); Maj. Gen. Holland M. Smith, USMC; Adm. Nimitz; V. Adm. Fitch, and Adm. Halsey. (Naval History and Heritage Command)

Major-General Collins, right, conferring with the commanding officer of 3rd Battalion, 27th Infantry Regiment on New Georgia. Collins was an outstanding leader, but his 25th Division played a fairly small role during the New Georgia campaign. (Official Marine Corps photo courtesy of Marine Corps History Division)

Admiral Halsey (seated in center, hatless) at a planning session on Bougainville with Marine Corps Major-Generals Allan H. Turnage and Roy S. Geiger in November 1943. (Naval History and Heritage Command)

On April 3, Yamamoto moved to Rabaul to set up an advanced headquarters to direct Operation *I*, his effort to reverse Japanese fortunes in the Solomons with a series of large air raids. After only four attacks, he declared the operation a success and brought it to an end on April 16. Days later, he was killed by aircraft from an airfield he believed was suppressed. This photo shows Yamamoto watching an A6M taking off as part of Operation *I*. (Juzo Nakamura via Lansdale Research Associates)

operation when **Major-General Charles D. Barrett**, USMC, commander of I Marine Amphibious Corps, was killed in an accident. **Major-General Roy S. Geiger**, USMC, another veteran of the Guadalcanal campaign, took over from Vandegrift on November 9. The 3rd Marine Division was commanded by **Major-General Allen H. Turnage**, USMC, who took over the division in the summer.

JAPANESE COMMANDERS

The conduct of Japanese operations throughout the Solomons campaign, and throughout the war, was handicapped by the inability of the IJN and the IJA to form a truly joint command. Both services were co-equals at Imperial General Headquarters; while the Army and Navy Sections of Imperial General Headquarters were successful in fostering some degree of cooperation for strategic operations, this did not result in a unified command at the operational level. However, the endemic friction between the two services was minimized in the Solomons by the close working relationship and friendship of the respective service commanders.

The Combined Fleet controlled Japanese naval forces in the Solomons. Commander of the Combined Fleet

was **Admiral Yamamoto Isoroku.** He had been in command of the Combined Fleet since August 1939 and had overseen the initial period of Japanese expansion. Since May 1942, when the IJN suffered its first defeat at Coral Sea, Yamamoto had suffered an unbroken string of reverses. His reputation as a brilliant leader is undeserved. Yamamoto's tenure as Commander of the Combined Fleet ended on April 18, 1943 when the aircraft he was riding in was shot down over southern Bougainville. His successor was **Admiral Koga Mineichi** who advocated a defensive strategy in the Solomons.

Once forces were detached from the Combined Fleet in Truk to fight in the Solomons, they were attached to the Southeastern Area Fleet headquartered at Rabaul. This force was led by **Vice Admiral Kusaka Jinichi.** He was known as an unusually aggressive commander, which was noteworthy since aggressiveness was the norm in the IJN. Kusaka had a difficult task since his force was charged to support operations in the Solomons and on New Guinea and because Koga was reluctant to commit forces from the Combined Fleet for operations in the South Pacific since he faced the prospect of an American advance in the Central Pacific led by Nimitz. Kusaka retained command of the Southeastern Area Fleet until the end of the war and was present at the surrender of Japanese forces at Rabaul on September 6, 1945.

The principal IJN force in the Solomons was the 8th Fleet under **Vice Admiral Mikawa Gunichi.** Mikawa was a proven combat commander who had led the 8th Fleet since July 1942. He had proved that Japanese island garrisons could be moved and supplied by Japanese destroyers moving at night to avoid American air power. He was relieved in April 1943 and succeeded by **Vice Admiral Samejima Tomoshige.** He retained this command until the end of the war when he surrendered to Australian troops on Bougainville on September 8, 1945.

Several IJN task group commanders distinguished themselves during the campaign. Foremost among these was **Rear Admiral Ijuin Matsuji**, Commander of Destroyer Squadron 3, who

ABOVE LEFT

General Imamura, Commander in Chief, Eighth Area Army, was responsible for conducting operations in the Solomons and eastern New Guinea. Unusually for an IJA officer, he was able to establish a close working relationship with his IJN counterpart. Nevertheless, he was defeated on New Guinea and in the Solomons and was destined to spend the remainder of the war in bypassed Rabaul. (Naval History and Heritage Command)

ABOVE RIGHT

General Hyakutake commanded the 17th Army responsible for operations in the Solomons. He failed at Guadalcanal even though he demonstrated imagination in developing his strategy, but failed to take into account the enemy or the terrain. He was destined to suffer the same fate on Bougainville. (Official Marine Corps photo courtesy of Marine Corps History Division)

fought several engagements during the campaign. All these officers possessed a wealth of combat experience, mainly during the Guadalcanal campaign, and benefited from the IJN extensive pre-war training.

While the IJA's air force operated almost exclusively over New Guinea, the IJN's air force was responsible for operations over the Solomons. This force consisted of the 11th Air Fleet (later designated the 1st Base Air Force) and was commanded by **Vice Admiral Kusaka Jinichi**, concurrently with his responsibility as Southeastern Area Fleet commander.

The IJA command responsible for operations in the Solomons, and eastern New Guinea, was the 8th Area Army led by **General Imamura Hitoshi**. He retained his command throughout the war and surrendered it in September 1945. Following the war, he was tried and convicted as a war criminal. Subordinate to this force were two field armies and an air division. The 17th Army, commanded by **General Hyakutake Harukichi** operated in the Solomons. Hyakutake took command of the 17th Army in May 1942 and was the loser of the Guadalcanal campaign, where he consistently underestimated the strength of the American garrison on the island. Despite this, he retained command of the 17th Army and continued to fight in the Solomons until February 1945 when he was incapacitated by a stroke on Bougainville.

At the operational level, the IJA had a wealth of tough, ultra-aggressive but largely inflexible commanders. The Japanese ground commander on New Georgia was **Major-General Sasaki Noboru** in his capacity as commander of the Southeastern Detachment. He fought well in the Central Solomons and escaped to Rabaul. The principal ground commander on Bougainville was **Major-General Kanda Masatane**, commander of the 6th Infantry Division since 1941. He assumed command of the 17th Army after Hyakutake's stroke in 1945 and surrendered it in September. He was tried and convicted of war crimes after the war.

OPPOSING FORCES

AMERICAN AND ALLIED FORCES

Naval Forces

The victorious US Navy paid a heavy price during the Guadalcanal campaign, losing 25 ships. This heavy attrition changed the way it approached the naval war in the Solomons through 1943. Major fleet units like carriers and the new fast battleships would now only be risked to screen major landings from the possibility of intervention by the Combined Fleet from Truk. The responsibilities for conducting surface bombardments, screening invasion forces, and intercepting Japanese surface forces conducting reinforcement and resupply runs was assigned to two mixed light cruiser–destroyer task forces. Each of these was typically assigned up to four light cruisers and up to eight destroyers. After a series of night engagements between these cruiser–destroyer forces and Japanese destroyer task forces in which the US Navy fared poorly, cruisers were withheld for use only in major operations.

Ships and weapons

At the start of the campaign, the US Navy still clung to the notion that big guns were the key to victory and built its night surface forces around cruisers. The principal class of light cruisers available at the start of the Solomons campaign was the pre-war Brooklyn class. Four of the nine ships in the class saw action in the Solomons. These were large ships with a full-load displacement of over 12,000 tons. They were armed with 15 6in./47 guns arranged in five triple turrets and eight dual-purpose 5in. guns. Top speed was a respectable 32.5 knots.

The standard US Navy light cruiser from mid-1943 was the Cleveland class. Ultimately, 27 were completed and several saw action in the Solomons. These ships were larger than the Brooklyns and topped 14,000 tons full load. They carried 12 6in./47 guns and

Nashville was a member of the very successful Brooklyn class of light cruisers. Note the five triple turrets mounting 15 6in. guns. *Nashville* made her combat debut in the Solomons on January 4, 1943 with a night bombardment of Munda Airfield. While shelling Vila Airfield on Kolombangara on May 12, the cruiser suffered an accidental explosion in one of her forward turrets which killed 18 and wounded 17. This view is from August 1943 following repairs and modernization. (Naval History and Heritage Command)

12 of the excellent 5in./38 dual-purpose guns. The ships could steam at a top speed of 32.5 knots. With their powerful main armament, excellent antiaircraft capabilities, and modern electronics, these were the most powerful light cruisers of the war.

The 6in./47 gun, mounted on the Brooklyn and Cleveland-classes, was an outstanding weapon, primarily because of its remarkable rate of fire. This was achieved by the use of semi-fixed ammunition which combined the shell with a brass cartridge containing the powder and primer. Maximum rate of fire was 8–12 rounds per minute firing a 130-pound shell. It proved effective both in an anti-ship and shore bombardment role.

Cleveland photographed while underway in late 1942. She was the lead ship of the largest and most powerful class of light cruisers ever built. The similarity of the Cleveland class to the Brooklyn class is obvious. The principal difference between the two is the elimination of one of the forward triple 6in. turrets in favor of a heavier secondary armament of 12 5in./38 guns in six twin mounts. (Naval History and Heritage Command)

American destroyers played an increasingly prominent role during the campaign. They operated in squadrons which were typically assigned two destroyer divisions each with four destroyers.

Pre-war American destroyers emphasized firepower and were built around a large torpedo battery of 8–16 21in. torpedo tubes and a 4–6 gun 5in./38 main battery. Unlike Japanese destroyers, American destroyers did not carry torpedo reloads.

Built in vast numbers, 175 by 1944, the first Fletcher-class destroyers began to reach the South Pacific in November 1942. These ships were excellent, well-rounded destroyers with a heavy armament, and possessed good speed (maximum 36.5 knots) and endurance. The ships carried five 5in./38 guns in single mounts and ten Mark 15 torpedoes. The reliability

Fletcher-class destroyer *Charles Ausburne* receiving mail by highline from light cruiser *Columbia* while steaming in the Solomon Islands, September 27, 1943. On the night of September 27–28, *Charles Ausburne* claimed two Japanese barges sunk off Vella Lavella. Note the SC and SG radars on the foremast and the Mk. 4 fire-control radar on the Mk. 37 director. (Naval History and Heritage Command)

problems of the Mark 15 torpedo had been solved by July 1943, but it had a fairly short effective range of 6,000 yards. By late 1943, the Fletcher class was carrying the bulk of the front-line duties in the Solomons.

Night-Fighting Doctrine and Capabilities

US Naval night-fighting doctrine in 1942 revolved around the premise that big guns were dominant, even at night. Therefore, night surface task groups were built around cruisers. Originally, these were heavy cruisers, since they had a greater ability to penetrate the armor of IJN cruisers and battleships, if present. Since the US Navy had no real idea of the true capabilities of the Japanese Type 93 torpedo, most heavy cruisers committed to night actions were sunk or damaged at some point in the Guadalcanal campaign. By 1943, the heavy cruisers were removed from night combat duties and replaced by light cruisers since their faster-firing 6in. guns were seen as more suitable for taking on Japanese destroyers. Coupled with radar, the Americans expected to smother a Japanese destroyer in 6in. fire before it could launch torpedoes. This proved illusory since, as explained below, there were problems with radar-guided gunfire. American admirals were convinced that they could effectively engage a target at 10,000 yards with radar-controlled gunnery which was beyond the range of Japanese torpedoes. This showed a total ignorance of the true capabilities of the Japanese Type 93 torpedo which had an effective range greater than 6in. cruiser guns.

American night combat doctrine was also totally ignorant of the potential of American torpedoes, which had proven largely ineffective during the Guadalcanal campaign. This was the result of pre-war night-fighting doctrine in which destroyers were almost totally subservient to cruisers. In 1942, US Navy destroyers were used to finish off cripples from cruiser gunfire or to screen the cruisers from destroyer attack. Accordingly, destroyers were tied to the cruisers and not allowed to operate independently. By August 1943, American commanders finally decided that their destroyers could do more than simply screen cruisers. By this point, defects in the Mark 15 destroyer-launched torpedo had finally been identified and corrected. When combined with radar, US Navy destroyers possessed considerable offensive power. For the last months of the campaign, destroyers bore the brunt of night surface combat against the Japanese.

Radar

Radar played a huge role in the night surface battles fought in the Solomons. This technological advantage blunted, and eventually surpassed, Japanese advantages in night fighting. By 1943, all US Navy destroyers and cruisers were equipped with surface-search and fire-control radars. Early American radars, the SC/SC-2, were unreliable and their operators and commanders did not fully understand how to integrate them into night combat. The SG surface-search radar reached the fleet in late 1942 and was the first American

This radar screen shot depicts the action in the Kula Gulf on March 6, 1943 when US Navy light cruisers sank two IJN destroyers. It shows the SG radarscope image on *Denver* just before the cruisers opened fire. It also shows the relative ease in interpreting a plan position indicator display. *Denver* is the bright spot in the center of the scope, with other US Navy ships ahead, heading southwesterly. The large white patch at left is Kolombangara with New Georgia on the right. The large spot just off Kolombangara is the Japanese destroyers *Minegumo* and *Murasame*, both of which were sunk in this action. (Naval History and Heritage Command)

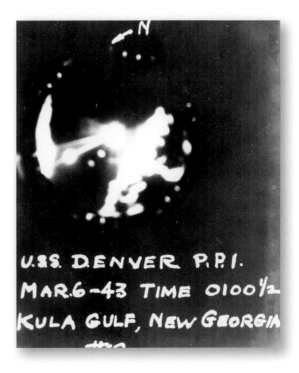

U.S.S. DENVER P.P.I.
MAR.6-43 TIME 0100½
KULA GULF, NEW GEORGIA

S-band radar. It was also the first surface search radar to use a plan position indicator display. This provided a radar "map" of the search area and was much easier to use and interpret. The range for the SG/SG-1 was highly dependent on atmospheric conditions, but could be as much as 15nm against a destroyer-sized target.

US Navy light cruisers were fitted with the Mark 3 fire-control radar; destroyers carried the Mark 4 fire-control radar. The use of radar was revolutionary for fire control, and had obvious advantages at night and in poor visibility conditions. However, the US Navy became over-confident in its abilities. The problem was the Mark 3 radar's inability to distinguish the original target from shell splashes once the target was engaged. This quickly decreased the accuracy of radar-controlled gunfire, since shell splashes in front of the target often provided the strongest radar returns which prompted the operator to target the splashes. This led to the phenomenon known as "chasing splashes," which made gunnery increasingly inaccurate as the real target moved away. When the firing ship finally stopped engaging its own shell splashes, the original target was gone, leading to the assessment that it had been sunk. When the original target was subsequently detected, it appeared as a new target, making it hard to get a true read on the size of an enemy force.

Air Forces

Allied air forces were under the control of Air Command Solomons (or AIRSOLS). This was a multi-service (Navy, Marine, and Army Air Force (AAF)) and multi-national (New Zealand) formation. Under Halsey's leadership, service friction was overcome and the AIRSOLS staff functioned at a high level on operational matters. However, Allied air forces operated under consistent logistical difficulties and fought under primitive conditions. On June 30, Fitch had under his command 533 combat aircraft of which 213 fighters, 170 bombers and attack aircraft, and 72 heavy bombers were

On February 12, the Marine Corps deployed its first F4U Corsair fighters in the Solomons. This represented a dramatic improvement over the F4F Wildcat in terms of speed and range and the Corsair played a central role in gaining Allied air superiority over the Solomons during the campaign. By the end of the campaign, the majority of the five Marine fighter squadrons in the Solomons were flying Corsairs. These Corsairs are operating from an airfield on the Russell Islands before the invasion of New Georgia. (Official Marine Corps photo courtesy of Marine Corps History Division)

operational. Throughout 1943, the weight of Allied air power in the Solomons greatly surpassed that of the Japanese.

AIRSOLS played the key role in the Allied drive up the Solomons since a prerequisite to any amphibious operation was to neutralize Japanese air power. No other major amphibious operations in the war up to this point had been conducted as closely to major Japanese air bases. AIRSOLS began pounding Japanese air bases in the Central Solomons and Bougainville in early 1943. Marine TBF Avengers and SBD Dauntlesses struck Munda, Vila, and Rekata Bay. Longer-ranged AAF B-24 and B-17 heavy bombers hit Ballale, Kahili, and the Buin area. Anti-shipping missions were flown by Marine Avengers and AAF B-25s flying up and down the Solomons looking for Japanese cargo ships, barges, or destroyers on resupply runs.

Allied air support during the New Georgia operation was generally good since there were several airfields within range to provide fighter cover. Fighter coverage was provided from 0700 to1630hrs over the island. Following a large Japanese air attack on July 15 against Rendova and New Georgia during which the Japanese incurred heavy casualties, they virtually stopped daylight air attacks against the invasion area and relied solely on night harassment attacks. The Marines introduced night-fighters, but these were in their infancy and proved largely ineffective.

During the campaign, the scale of Allied air support provided to ground troops grew. Most of these missions were flown by Marine squadrons using Avengers and Dauntlesses. Almost all were flown against targets well away

At the start of the campaign, the mainstay American fighter in the Solomons was the F4F Wildcat flown by Marine and Navy squadrons. With a combat radius of some 200 miles, Wildcats flying from Guadalcanal (like the ones shown here) had a limited loiter time over the Central Solomons. (Official Marine Corps photo courtesy of Marine Corps History Division)

For most of the Solomons campaign, the Marines flew three dive-bomber squadrons equipped with the SBD Dauntless. These were capable maritime strike and ground support aircraft. By the end of the campaign on Bougainville, Marine aircraft were dropping 100-pound bombs within 75 yards of friendly troops. (Official Marine Corps photo courtesy of Marine Corps History Division)

The TBF Avenger was flown by three Marine squadrons during the campaign. Like the Dauntless dive-bombers, the Avenger performed maritime strike and ground support missions, but the Avenger carried a heavier 2,000-pound payload in its internal bomb bay. This Marine Avenger pictured is actually a 1945 aircraft flying over Okinawa. (Official Marine Corps photo courtesy of Marine Corps History Division)

from the front line. Though in direct support of the ground offensive, this did not represent true close air support. The few times close air support was conducted in the Central Solomons, it proved dangerous and at times fatal for friendly ground troops. On Bougainville, the Marines began to develop the tactics which eventually led to routine and effective close air support.

Once Munda was taken, it became the most used airfield in the South Pacific. In October, Twining shifted the focus of AIRSOLS operations to reduce the Japanese airfields on Bougainville in advance of the landing at Cape Torokina on November 1. The Allies were flying from facilities on Ondonga Island, Segi, and Munda on New Georgia, the Russell Islands, and from the several airfields on Guadalcanal. Japanese airfields proved able to take a remarkable degree of punishment, but by mid-October the Japanese were finding it difficult to maintain aircraft on Bougainville and most aircraft were pulled back to Rabaul. For the landing at Empress Augusta Bay, air cover over the amphibious force consisted primarily of P-38s at high altitude and F4Us at lower levels. This was sufficient to protect the landing force against fairly large air attacks and took an increasing toll of Japanese aircraft.

AIRSOLS used a wide array of combat aircraft. The Marines flew F4U Corsairs and F4F Wildcat fighters. The former was superior to the standard Japanese fighter of the period (the A6M "Zero") and the Wildcat could more than hold its own if it used tactics suited for it. The Marines also flew TBF-1 Avenger torpedo bombers and SBD-3 Dauntless dive-bombers for ground support and maritime strike. The Navy contributed some of its first F6F Hellcat squadrons for the Central Solomons campaign. The Hellcat was also superior to the Japanese Zero fighter. The 13th Air Force was the Army element within AIRSOLS; it flew a mix of outdated P-39 and P-40 single-engine fighters and the long-range twin-engine P-38 fighter. One of the best medium bombers of the war, the B-25 was also present, as were B-17 and B-24 heavy bombers. The Royal New Zealand Air Force flew three squadrons of P-40 fighters.

Ground Forces

US Army forces in the South Pacific were considerable. By mid-1943, there were a total of 275,000 Army personnel present, including combat, air forces, and service troops. The principal ground units were four infantry divisions. The American and 25th Divisions had both fought on Guadalcanal and thus had some combat experience. The 43rd Division had no combat experience but was used to invade the Russell Islands in February 1943 so had at least some experience with amphibious operations. This was the unit selected to lead the invasion of New Georgia. The final division, the 37th, was also untested in combat since it had been committed to garrison duty on the Fiji Islands since 1942.

The 37th and 43rd Divisions were both National Guard units which generally had a lower level of training and were commanded by an officer cadre with a lower level of professionalism compared to regular army units.

The US Army infantry division of the period was a large formation with a total assigned strength of 14,666 men. It was organized into three infantry regiments, each with a strength of 3,323 men in three infantry battalions. Each regiment was heavily armed with 24 37mm antitank guns, 18 81mm and 27

60mm mortars, and 52 light and heavy machine guns. The backbone of the division was the 2,410-man artillery regiment with its four artillery battalions. Three battalions were equipped with the excellent M2A1 105mm howitzer (12 per battalion), and the fourth, acting in a general support role, was equipped with 12 M1918 155mm howitzers. American artillery fire control was of the highest order and allowed massive firepower to be brought quickly to bear anywhere in the division's sector. American logistics capabilities ensured that the artillery was provided with lavish amounts of ammunition.

In addition to US Army ground combat troops, the US Marine Corps was also present in the South Pacific. Two Marine divisions, one raider regiment, six defense battalions, and one parachute regiment were under the command of the I Marine Amphibious Corps. Some of these units saw action in the Central Solomons, but the bulk of I Marine Amphibious Corps was withheld

The standard US Army howitzer during the war was the M2A1 105mm weapon which equipped three of the four artillery battalions in an infantry division. The howitzer could throw a 33-pound shell out to 12,200 yards. (Official Marine Corps photo courtesy of Marine Corps History Division)

The M1918 155mm howitzer, which equipped the medium artillery battalion in US Army infantry divisions, was a French design from World War I. Lightly modernized, it served into World War II until the more capable M1 155mm could be produced in sufficient quantities. The M1918 could throw a 100-pound shell over 12,300 yards. (Official Marine Corps photo courtesy of Marine Corps History Division)

The primary Marine artillery piece on Bougainville was the 75mm M1A1 pack howitzer. It had a range of 9,610 yards, but could also be used in a direct-fire mode since it was small enough to manhandle on the battlefield. (Official Marine Corps photo courtesy of Marine Corps History Division)

for the landing on Bougainville. The centerpiece of the force was the 3rd Marine Division. Bougainville was the first combat action for the division. It had been established on September 16, 1942 from cadres supplied by the 2nd Marine Division. Despite having no combat experience, the division was well-trained for rapid offensive maneuvers and possessed the high morale common to Marine units.

The April 1943 establishment for a Marine division called for a large formation of 1,041 Marine and Navy officers and 18,924 Marine and Navy enlisted men. The division was built around three infantry regiments, each with 148 officers and 3,094 enlisted men in three infantry battalions each with 38 officers and 915 enlisted men. Among the division's organic support units was a tank battalion with 54 light tanks, a weapons battalion with a company of antiaircraft and three companies of antitank guns, an amphibious tractor battalion, and a large engineer unit with over 2,500 officers and men. The organic artillery regiment was organized into five battalions. Three were equipped with 75mm pack howitzers (12 each), and two with 105mm howitzers (12 each).

Marine Raider battalions also fought in the Solomons. They were smaller and less well equipped with heavy weapons than a typical Marine infantry battalion. In March 1943, the four existing Raider battalions were organized into the 1st Raider Regiment. The establishment for each was set at four rifle companies and a weapons company. They were trained as lightly equipped infantry designated for special tasks, but could fill in as regular infantry if required. The 1st and 4th Raider Battalions saw action on New Georgia; the 2nd and 3rd Raiders were assigned to the 2nd Marine Raider Regiment (Provisional) and fought on Bougainville.

Marine parachute battalions were organized and trained similarly to Raider units. The 1st Marine Parachute Regiment saw action with its three subordinate battalions on Bougainville.

JAPANESE FORCES

Naval Forces

The Eighth Fleet, based at Rabaul, was assigned the responsibility of contesting the American advance in the Solomons. While Japanese strategy in the Solomons was strategically defensive, it did call for immediate local counterattacks wherever the Americans landed. This required the IJN to move ground forces under heavy air threat to various islands. In reality, this translated to IJN destroyers continuing their operations to transport, reinforce, and supply the Japanese garrisons in the Solomons.

The Guadalcanal campaign was very costly for the IJN, which lost 18 ships including two battleships and four cruisers. When the Americans began their drive up the Solomons, the IJN decided not to contest it with the main body of the Combined Fleet in order to preserve it for a future decisive battle with the US Navy. Therefore, the burden of supporting Japanese garrisons in the Central and Northern Solomons fell upon the Combined Fleet's destroyer squadrons. Destroyers had proven very effective at Guadalcanal since they were able to use their speed to move at night to conduct supply and reinforcements missions, thus evading Allied air attack. When the US Navy attempted to interdict the supply runs with surface forces, the IJN's well-trained and heavily armed destroyers were more than able to hold their own. By 1943, the Japanese destroyer force was losing its fine edge due to losses and heavy use, but it was still ideally suited for operations in the Solomons and performed well during the campaign.

Myoko was the lead ship in the IJN's first class of "Treaty" cruisers. Commissioned in 1929, the ship had established a fine war record by late 1943. She was one of only two IJN heavy cruisers to survive the war. (Naval History and Heritage Command)

The Japanese reluctance to commit major forces to the Central Solomons extended even to its destroyer force. This required the Eighth Fleet to fight a poor-man's war even though the Combined Fleet maintained large forces at Truk, only some 800 miles north of Rabaul. The Eighth Fleet was also charged with supporting Japanese operations on New Guinea, which further taxed its slender resources. In March 1943, it was assigned fleet flagship heavy cruiser *Chokai* and Destroyer Squadron 3. This squadron was assigned light cruiser *Sendai* and Destroyer Divisions 11, 22, 30. Throughout the

Jintsu photographed in 1924–25; the ship retained the same basic configuration in 1943, but the catapult was moved from in front of the forward superstructure to a position abaft the last stack. The three ships of the Naka class were designed as leaders for destroyer squadrons and modernized before the war to carry Type 93 torpedoes. Two ships in the class, *Sendai* and *Jintsu* fought in the Solomons and both were lost to US Navy 6in. gunfire. (Naval History and Heritage Command)

Amagiri, seen here in a 1930s photograph, was a member of the "Special Type" destroyer class that was the most heavily armed in the world when they entered service in 1928. The ships carried six 5in. guns in three twin-gun mounts and three triple torpedo mounts. Of the 19 ships in the class at the start of the war, 14 fought in the Solomons. *Amagiri* was very active during the Solomons campaign taking part in the battles of Kula Gulf and Cape St. George and conducting many supply and reinforcement run. In August, she rammed and sank *PT-109*, then commanded by future president of the United States, John F. Kennedy. (Naval History and Heritage Command)

campaign, the Japanese fed reinforcements into Rabaul. In July, Destroyer Squadron 2 was committed followed by several destroyer divisions in August. In October 1943, Sentai 5 (a unit comprised of heavy cruisers) and Destroyer Squadron 10 were committed to the Eighth Fleet.

Each destroyer squadron was assigned a light cruiser as its flagship and up to four destroyer divisions. Each division was supposed to have 3–4 ships, but by the middle of 1943 attrition and the requirement for overhauls following incessant operations from austere forward bases had reduced a typical division to 1–2 destroyers.

IJN Ships and Weapons

Japanese heavy cruisers were formidable ships. Since the IJN did not bother to adhere to the pre-war treaty restrictions, their heavy cruisers were larger and more powerful than comparable US Navy ships. The Myoko class, which fought late in the campaign, displaced almost 16,000 tons full load, and carried 10 8in. guns and 16 24in. torpedo tubes. Japanese light cruisers were designed to act as flagships for destroyer squadrons and thus were smaller and much less heavily armed than US Navy light cruisers. IJN light cruisers of the Nagara and Sendai classes displaced 7,200–7,600 tons full load and carried seven 5.5in. guns in single mounts and eight torpedo tubes.

Japanese destroyers were exceptional ships for conducting surface warfare. However, they were not well-rounded warships since their antiair and antisubmarine capabilities were marginal, but this did not matter during night combat in the Solomons. Several classes of Japanese destroyers fought in the Solomons. The Fubuki class was the world's most powerful when

Most of the IJN's follow-on destroyer classes were broadly similar in size and capabilities to the Special Type destroyers. The 19 ships of the Kagero class entered service between 1939 and 1941; of these, 17 fought at some point in the Solomons in 1942–43. This is *Yukikaze*, photographed in 1940, which fought at the Battle of Kolombangara and conducted many supply runs during the campaign while suffering no damage. (Naval History and Heritage Command)

it entered service in 1927 by virtue of its heavy gun armament of six 5in. guns and impressive torpedo battery of nine 24in. torpedo tubes. The follow-on classes of destroyers (the Shiratsuyu, Asashio, Kagero, and Yugumo classes), employed the same basic capabilities but with only eight torpedo tubes. The Akitsuki class of large destroyers was maximized for antiaircraft screening, but still carried eight 3.9in. guns and four torpedo tubes. Unlike US Navy destroyers, all IJN destroyers carried reloads for their torpedo tubes. A well-trained crew could reload torpedoes in about 15 minutes.

The bedrock of IJN night fighting capabilities was the Type 93 torpedo. Officially adopted in 1933 (the year 2593 on the Japanese calendar), it was an extraordinary weapon and was the finest torpedo in the world. The secret to its long-range (21,900 yards at 48 knots) and large (1,078 pound) warhead was its oxygen-powered propulsion system. It was fitted on all heavy cruisers, select light cruisers, and eventually all modern IJN destroyers. Because the Japanese treated it as top secret, its existence was unknown to the US Navy at the start of the war and it was not until late 1943 that the Americans realized its true capabilities and took measures to counter it.

The IJN's Type 93 torpedo, carried aboard cruisers and destroyers, was the dominant factor in many of the night clashes in the Solomons. This is a Type 93 on exhibit in Washington, DC during World War II after having been recovered from a reef off Guadalcanal. (Naval History and Heritage Command)

Japanese Night-Fighting Doctrine

The Japanese placed great emphasis on developing and exercising night-fighting doctrine and tactics. The 1934 Battle Instructions underscored the importance of destroyer squadrons in night combat. Each destroyer squadron was supported by a division of heavy cruisers to make up a night combat group. The heavy cruisers provided the combat power to permit the destroyers to penetrate to attack the enemy's battleships. By 1936, night combat was seen as an essential part of the planned decisive battle against the US Navy. In a carefully choreographed sequence, IJN heavy cruisers would open the battle with a massed torpedo assault. The action culminated with a massed attack by the destroyer squadrons at close range. The destroyers would fire their first torpedo load, then disengage, reload, and fire a second barrage. There were no major fleet engagements in the Solomons of the kind the IJN spent the pre-war years practicing for, but many of the elements of IJN pre-war night combat doctrine was applicable to naval warfare as it unfolded during the campaign.

Doctrine was useful as a general guide for night combat, but Japanese commanders modified it during the Solomons campaign. The Japanese were fully aware of the American use of radar. Not wanting to be surprised by the Americans, and especially after the battle of Vella Gulf, where American destroyers surprised and torpedoed three Japanese destroyers before the Japanese were even aware of the presence of the Americans, later in the campaign Japanese commanders would fire their torpedoes as soon as they gained contact with the enemy and could get a fire solution. Following that, the Japanese would move out of range to reload torpedoes and then seek to re-engage. Gunfire was not favored, but was used immediately if surprised. Japanese guns also used smokeless powder to avoid disclosing the location.

Japanese Radar

The IJN had a very limited number of ships equipped with radar, at least until mid-1943 when select Japanese destroyers finally received the No. 22 radar designed for surface search. Against a destroyer-sized target, the No. 22 was supposedly effective out to approximately 9nm. However, it was unreliable and Japanese operators often poorly trained. In order to compensate for the lack of radar, the Japanese had to rely on their superior optics, like the Type 88 Model 1 night binoculars introduced in 1932. These were superior to American optics and often out-performed radar. Additionally, in 1943 the IJN widely deployed radar detectors. Because of the dynamics of radar energy, radar detectors could provide an awareness of the presence of a US Navy ship using radar before the same US Navy ship could achieve radar detection. The IJN did not use radar for fire control and the lack of a modern radar system put the IJN in a very perilous position during night engagements, which was the single most important factor in many of the night battles fought in the Solomons.

Air Forces

At the start of the New Georgia campaign, on June 30, the 11th Air Fleet based at Rabaul had 83 fighters and 66 bombers of all types. These were the cream of the IJN's land-based air units. Following the heavy air losses suffered in the Guadalcanal campaign, the IJN's air force found itself in a difficult position. It was forced to send a constant flow of reinforcements to Rabaul to maintain the strength of the units there which were under constant attacks from Allied air units under both Halsey's and MacArthur's commands. The diversion to Rabaul of the Combined Fleet's carrier air groups for Yamamoto's Operation *I* in April temporarily increased the strength of IJN air power in South Pacific up to 350 aircraft. This powerful force conducted a number of raids against targets on Guadalcanal and New Guinea, but these were largely ineffective. The carrier aircraft were withdrawn to Truk after a 15 percent loss rate in only two weeks. Later during the battle for New Georgia, aircraft from one of the Combined Fleet's carrier divisions were sent to bases in Buin on Bougainville. In two weeks, one-third of the aircraft and pilots were lost and the air groups were withdrawn.

By 1943, the IJN's A6M Zero had lost its technological edge over the most recent generation of American fighters. Nevertheless, the Zero was forced to remain in front-line service until the end of the war since no suitable replacement was ever developed. This is a Zero captured on Munda airfield. (Official Marine Corps photo courtesy of Marine Corps History Division)

NEW GEORGIA **USMC PHOTO NO.19**

NEW GEORGIA   USMC PHOTO   No.11–18

The Japanese air war over the Solomons was almost exclusively fought by the IJN. The IJA Air Force (IJAAF) concentrated on the air war over New Guinea, and made only occasional appearances in the Central Solomons. This is an IJAAF Ki-48 Lily light bomber found on Munda Airfield after its capture. (Official Marine Corps photo courtesy of Marine Corps History Division)

With the IJA's air force in the South Pacific dedicated to the fight on New Guinea, the only real source of reinforcement for the hard-pressed 11th Air Fleet was the Combined Fleet's carrier air groups on Truk. These had some of the most proficient airmen left in the IJN. Koga did not want to weaken his prospects for a possible fleet engagement, so resisted calls from Kusaka to return the carrier aircraft to the South Pacific. In late September, Koga led the Combined Fleet from Truk to attack the US Navy's carrier force, but the intelligence that the operation was based on was faulty, so no battle took place. In October, Koga relented and plans were made for the commitment of the Combined Fleet's carrier air groups to Rabaul for ten days.

The aircraft arrived at Rabaul on November 1 and 2. The addition of the 173 carrier aircraft (82 fighters, 45 dive-bombers, 40 torpedo bombers, and six reconnaissance aircraft) joined the approximately 200 aircraft of the 11th Air Fleet. These were used to attack the US Navy landing at Cape Torokina, and in the process suffered heavy losses. The official Japanese history of the war placed these losses at 70 percent of the aircraft and 47 percent of the crews committed. This attrition to an irreplaceable asset had long-lasting strategic impact. Without an effective carrier force, the IJN could not interfere with the US Navy landing in the Gilbert Islands in November. It took the IJN many months to rebuild its carrier air groups, and this process was not fully finished even by June 1944 when the Combined Fleet was committed in a decisive battle against the US Navy's carrier force off the Marianas and suffered a shattering defeat.

In 1943, the IJN was still using the same aircraft it began the war with. The standard IJN fighter, both carrier and land-based, was the A6M Type 0. The Allies gave it the reporting name "Zeke" but it was most often referred to as the "Zero." The Zero possessed exceptional range and low-speed maneuverability, making it a deadly dog-fighter, but compared to modern Allied fighters, it was deficient in armament, protection, high-altitude performance, and higher-speed maneuverability. With a well-trained pilot,

The G4M Betty was the IJN's standard land-based long-range bomber before the war. By 1943, it was generally restricted to night operations because of its demonstrated vulnerability to interception. This is a destroyed Betty on Munda airfield in August 1943. (Naval History and Heritage Command)

the Zero remained a formidable adversary, but fewer and fewer Japanese pilots were as well trained as their Allied adversaries. The IJN's standard dive-bomber was the D3A2 "Val" which was rugged and an accurate bombing platform, but it was slow and therefore vulnerable to interception. The standard torpedo bomber was the B5N2 "Kate" which was even more vulnerable than the Val in contested air space. The land-based two-engine G4M1/2 Type 1 Attack Bomber (called "Betty" by the Allies), was the standard IJN long-range bomber. It had a very long range, but was shockingly vulnerable to interception and was thus used increasingly in a night-attack role. By this point in the war, the level of training for Japanese pilots, even the elite carrier-based ones, had been drastically reduced. This was shown throughout the Solomons campaign when Zero pilots were routinely bested by Allied fighter pilots and IJN strike aircraft often failed to press home attacks on US Navy ships, and most often missed their target when they did.

Ground Forces

By early 1943, the IJA had just suffered its first ground defeat of the war against a western force on Guadalcanal. A highly trained and motivated infantry force deficient in fire power was bested by a US Marine and Army force which refused to be cowed by Japanese night attacks. Fighting spirit came in second to American firepower. The IJA had proved deficient in several key areas—planning major operations, combined-arms combat, intelligence, and logistics. None of this changed during the Solomons campaign—the IJA still underestimated the Americans, brought no armor to bear and still used basic artillery tactics. Most of all, the IJN proved unable to adequately supply the Army's island garrisons so it was continually faced with executing operations on a logistical shoestring.

Though the IJA saw defensive operations as detrimental to morale, its tenacious and brave soldiers proved excellent defensive fighters. In the attack, the Japanese almost always preferred night combat since this supposedly maximized the effect of Japanese fighting spirit and minimized the effects of American firepower. The preferred attack method was to mount a single or double flank attack in concert with pressure on the enemy's front. This was difficult to fully coordinate at night and in dense terrain like that found on the islands of the South Pacific. Nevertheless, determined infantry could almost always achieve some degree of tactical success by using infiltration tactics at night. The problem came the next day when these forces were unsupported by artillery and exposed to American counterattack.

The IJA task-organized units for particular missions. The basis for a force used for independent operations, like those in the Solomons, was an infantry regiment. This was supported by artillery, antitank, antiaircraft, and engineer units as required. The infantry regiment was a powerful unit with three large battalions each with 1,100 officers and men. The battalion was organized into four infantry companies and a heavy weapons company with 12 heavy machine guns and a gun company with four 70mm infantry guns. At the regimental level, there were another six 75mm infantry guns and 37mm antitank guns. There were no mortars; these were all grouped into independent battalions. Overall, the firepower of an IJA battalion, regiment, or division paled in comparison to that of a comparable US Marine or Army unit.

The 6th Infantry Division, commanded by Lt. Gen. Kanda Masatane, was the best unit in the 17th Army. It was one of the IJA's oldest units having been activated in 1870. From mid-1937, it fought in China so was combat experienced when it arrived in the Solomons. The unit was comprised of the 13th, 23rd, and 45th Infantry Regiments. The 13th was badly battered on New Georgia, but the other two regiments were at full strength for operations on Bougainville. The division's 6th Field Artillery Regiment was equipped with 36 75mm guns.

The 38th Infantry Division was shattered on Guadalcanal. It was partially re-formed after its remnants were withdrawn from the island in February 1943. The entire 229th Infantry Regiment fought on New Georgia. One of its battalions constituted the original garrison on Munda, arriving there in November 1942. The other two battalions were rebuilt following their evacuation from Guadalcanal. One was manned by reservists, and the other was never brought back to full strength. Elements of the 38th Division's 230th Infantry Regiment also fought on New Georgia. Units from the 17th Infantry Division fought on Bougainville. This division was comprised of the 53rd, 54th, and 81st Infantry Regiments.

The IJN contributed ground troops to the defense of the Solomons. The 8th Combined Special Naval Landing Force (SNLF) was activated in November 1942 and committed to the Central Solomons before the American invasion. The SNLF is often compared to the US Marines, but this comparison is entirely erroneous since the Japanese version was a defensive unit. Two formations comprised the 8th Combined SNLF—the Kure 6th and the Yokosuka 7th. These were battalion-sized units heavy on firepower and light on infantry. Each possessed two rifle companies comprised of barely-trained recruits, a heavy weapons company, antiaircraft units, and an assortment of naval artillery on fixed mounts.

NEW GEORGIA   USMC PHOTO   NO.7

Japanese ground forces relied on the deployment of well-trained infantry, not the employment of heavy firepower. The scale of heavy weapons in an IJA unit did not compare favorably with its US Army or Marine counterpart. For example, a Japanese infantry regiment possessed only six 37mm antitank guns, like the one shown here destroyed on New Georgia with its crew lying dead around it. (Official Marine Corps photo courtesy of Marine Corps History Division)

ORDERS OF BATTLE, JUNE 30, 1943

JAPANESE

Naval Forces

Eighth Fleet (Rabaul)—V. Adm. Samejima Tomoshige
Heavy cruiser *Chokai*
Light cruiser *Yubari*
Eight destroyers

Air Forces

Imperial Japanese Navy
11th Air Fleet (later designated 1st Base Air Force), V. Adm. Kusaka
  Jinichi
    25th Air Flotilla
    26th Air Flotilla
Operational Aircraft: 71 A6M2/3 Zero fighters, 38 G4M Betty bombers,
  11 D3A2 Val dive-bombers, four reconnaissance planes

Imperial Japanese Army
6th Air Division (Lt. Gen. Itabana Giichi)
    14th Air Brigade
        14th Regiment (Ki-21 heavy bombers)
        68th Regiment (Ki-61 fighters)
        78th Regiment (in transit, Ki-61 fighters)
About 50 operational aircraft

Ground Forces

Imperial Japanese Army
Southeastern Detachment (Maj. Gen. Sasaki Noboru)
    229th Infantry Regiment, 38th Infantry Division (Col. Hirata
      Genjiro)
        1st Battalion (Maj. Hara Masao); rebuilt but with only 2 infantry
          companies and a machine-gun company; located at Wickham
          and Viru Harbor
        2nd Battalion (Maj. Sato Giichi); full strength; located at Munda
        3rd Battalion (Maj. Kojima Bunzo); full strength, but rebuilt with
          reservists; located at Vila
    13th Infantry Regiment, 6th Infantry Division (Col. Tomonari
      Satoshi); all battalions full strength; located at Vila
        1st Battalion (Maj. Kinoshita Seishu)
        2nd Battalion (Maj. Obashi Takeo)
        3rd Battalion (Maj. Takabayashi Uichi)
    15th Field Antiaircraft Regiment—Munda and Vila

Imperial Japanese Navy
    8th Combined Special Naval Landing Force
    Kure 6th; located at Bairoko
    Yokosuka 7th; located on Kolombangara

UNITED STATES

Naval Forces

Third Fleet (Adm. William F. Halsey)
Task Force 31 Amphibious Force (R. Adm. Richmond K. Turner)
    Task Group 31.1 Western Group
        Rendova Attack Unit—four destroyer-transports
        Transport Unit—six transports, eight destroyers
    Task Group 31.3 Eastern Group
        Viru Occupation Unit—four destroyer-transports
        Task Unit 31.3.2 Segi Occupation Unit—various small craft
        Wickham Anchorage Occupation Group—three destroyer-
          transports

Task Force 36 (Adm. William F. Halsey)
    Task Group 36.1 (R. Adm. Walden L. Ainsworth)
        Three light cruisers, five destroyers
    Task Group 36.2 (R. Adm. A. Stanton Merrill)
        Four light cruisers, four destroyers, four minelayers
    Support Group C (R. Adm. DeWitt C. Ramsey)
    Two aircraft carriers; two light antiaircraft cruisers, four destroyers

Air Forces

Task Force 33, Air Force South Pacific (V. Adm. Aubrey W. Fitch)
    Solomons Island Air Force (R. Adm. Marc Mitscher)
    Fighter Command (Col. E. L. Pugh, USMC)
        258 fighters (213 operational; 65 F4U, 17 P-38, 72 F4F, 47 P-40,
          12 P-39)
    Strike Command (Col. C. F. Schilt, USMC)
        193 attack aircraft (170 operational; 77 SBD, 72 TBF, 21 B-25)
    Bomber Command (Brig. Gen G. C. Jamison, AAF)
        82 heavy bombers (72 operational; 9 B-17, 63 B-24)
    Search, utility, reconnaissance aircraft—48

Ground Forces

New Georgia Occupation Force (Maj. Gen. Hester)
43rd Infantry Division
    103rd Infantry Regiment
    169th Infantry Regiment
    172nd Infantry Regiment
9th Marine Defense Battalion
1st Marine Raider Regiment (less one battalion)
136th Field Artillery Battalion with 155mm howitzers (from 37th
    Division)
70th Coast Artillery Battalion (Antiaircraft), elements
One and one-half naval construction battalions
1st Commando, Fiji Guerillas (elements)

OPPOSING PLANS

AMERICAN PLANS

The basic premise of American planning for the campaign was the requirement to advance up the Solomons to seize airfields. Once airpower was in place in the northern Solomons, Rabaul could be isolated and then eventually captured. Given the range of American aircraft, primarily fighters, it was necessary to seize Bougainville Island in the northern Solomons to strike Rabaul with sufficient weight of air power to neutralize it. Halsey was responsible for guiding the planning effort and he understood the danger of exposing US Navy shipping to land-based Japanese air attack without being adequately covered by friendly land-based aircraft. It was impossible to simply land on Bougainville directly without the use of aircraft carriers. This was impossible since Halsey did not want to risk the US Navy's few remaining carriers against Japanese land-based air power. The alternative was to seize an airfield in the Central Solomons and use it to cover a landing on Bougainville.

The obvious choice for Halsey was to seize the airfield on Munda Point on New Georgia in the Central Solomons. This airfield was completed by the Japanese on December 15, 1942. After completing the airfield at Munda, the Japanese began work on another airfield at Vila on the nearby island of Kolombangara. Just as the airfield on Guadalcanal made that island the focal point for both sides during the first phase of the Solomons campaign, the locations of these two new airfields became the foci for the second phase.

The actual planning for the new offensive could not begin in earnest until March 1943. On March 12, a series of meetings commenced in Washington which guided the course of the Pacific War for the remainder of 1943. Representatives from both MacArthur's and Nimitz' commands were present, but MacArthur's representative, his Chief of Staff Maj. Gen. Richard K. Sutherland, had the responsibility of presenting the plan codenamed *Elkton*. The plan was basically the same scheme of maneuver from July 1942 and it was broken down into five operations: capture of airfields on the Huon Peninsula in New Guinea; capture of the airfield at Munda Point; capture of airfields on Bougainville and New Britain; capture of Kavieng to isolate Rabaul; finally, the capture of Rabaul itself. Timing of the operations was flexible, but it was generally assumed that Rabaul could be seized in 1943.

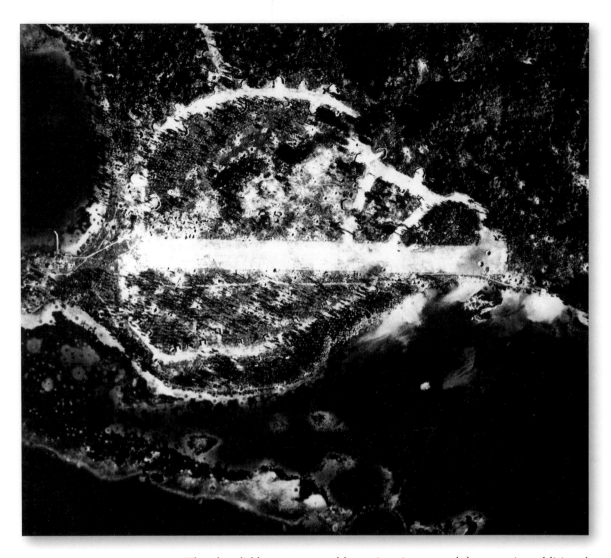

The Japanese airfield on Munda on New Georgia Island was the focal point of the Central Solomons campaign. Note the bomb craters from the constant American efforts to neutralize the airfield. (Official Marine Corps photo courtesy of Marine Corps History Division)

The plan did have some problems since it assumed that massive additional forces would be made available—five divisions, 45 air groups, and large numbers of warships and transports. Since this was clearly not possible in 1943, the plan had to be modified. A more realistic option was to seize only the southeastern part of Bougainville to capture the necessary airfields and to land on Cape Gloucester in western New Britain. In addition, Woodlark and Kiriwina Islands in the Trobriand Islands south of Rabaul were slated for capture to bring Rabaul into fighter and medium bomber range. The big change was that phase three, the capture of Rabaul, would be deferred to 1944. This modified scheme was the basis for the Joint Chiefs of Staff directive of March 28, 1943.

JAPANESE PLANS

The Guadalcanal campaign placed Japan clearly on the strategic defensive in the Pacific. Japan's advance into the South Pacific was decisively halted, but the Japanese wanted to hold their South Pacific positions to protect the major fleet base at Truk in the central Pacific and the Philippines, which lay astride Japan's SLOCs with the occupied Dutch East Indies. The key to the Japanese defenses in the south was Rabaul. As determined as the Americans were to take it, the Japanese were just as determined to hold it.

Japanese planning in the South Pacific in the aftermath of the evacuation of Guadalcanal in early February 1943 was disrupted by the continuing friction between the IJN and the IJA. There was no debate on the necessity of holding Rabaul; the debate was over how to do it. As early as November 1942, the Army and the Navy agreed to split up the theater with the Navy taking primary responsibility for the Solomons and the Army taking New Guinea.

In the aftermath of defeat at Guadalcanal, the Japanese decided to shift their primary effort from the Solomons to New Guinea. Mounting an "active defense" in the Solomons would permit forces to be used on New Guinea for offensive operations. Accordingly, all or parts of three IJA divisions were allocated to holding key point along the northern coast of New Guinea.

Operations in the Solomons were affected by another example of the IJN and IJA fighting separate wars in the same area. Imperial Headquarters gave orders that both the central and northern Solomons be defended. However, the IJA, fresh off its experience at Guadalcanal where a force of over two divisions was moved to the island and then not adequately supplied, wanted to defend the Solomons at Bougainville. With justification, it believed that supplying forces in the central Solomons would be too difficult. The IJN wanted to hold New Georgia in the central Solomons to provide depth to the defense of Bougainville. On March 22, the IJA and IJN reached an agreement that laid down how the Solomons would be defended. The IJA had responsibility for the Northern Solomons, and the IJN for the Central; however, the agreement provided for local commanders placing IJA units under IJN control for operations in the Central Solomons. Accordingly, the IJA positioned the 17th Army's 6th Division on Bougainville and adjacent islands, and in March 1943 the IJN sent the 8th Combined Special Naval Landing Force (SNLF) to New Georgia.

The small ground forces allocated to the Central Solomons were clearly inadequate, so the IJN quickly turned to the IJA for more troops. After negotiations between Kusaka and Imamura, and in the spirit of the March 22 agreement, the 17th Army sent the Southeastern Detachment to Kolombangara and New Georgia from May–July. This command, built around two battalions of the 229th Infantry Regiment and the entire 13th Infantry Regiment from the fresh 6th Division, was placed under the command of Maj. Gen. Sasaki Noboru. In an unusual development, the Southeastern Detachment was placed under the command of Samejima's Eighth Fleet from the onset of the campaign. On New Georgia, the defense of Munda was assigned to the IJA, and the IJN was assigned responsibility for the Enogai and Bairoko areas.

THE CAMPAIGN

OPENING MOVES

On the aftermath of the completion of the Guadalcanal campaign, both sides turned their attention to the Central Solomons. The start of the American invasion was delayed twice, first from April 1 to May 15, and then again to June 30. In the interim, the Japanese successfully moved ground forces to reinforce their positions on Munda on New Georgia and Vila on Kolombangara. American airpower pounded the airfields on Munda and Vila incessantly and the Japanese worked just as hard to keep them useable. In March, Halsey ordered Merrill to take his surface ships and bombard the two airfields. Four destroyers were sent against Munda, and a much larger force of three light cruisers and three destroyers was assigned to neutralize Vila. Merrill's cruiser force encountered and totally surprised two IJN destroyers in the early hours of March 6 inside Kula Gulf and made quick work of both. Merrill then proceeded to execute a short bombardment of both airfields. A further American effort to restrict Japanese reinforcement of the Central Solomons was a mining offensive conducted by aircraft and minelayers. Overall, the campaign was unsuccessful, but during the night of May 7–8, American mines laid in the Blackett Strait accounted for another two Japanese destroyers and heavily damaged a third.

Destroyers of Task Force 18 steam in column on May 13, 1943 after conducting a bombardment of Vila Airfield and Bairoko on New Georgia the night before. Extensive efforts by naval and air forces neutralized Vila and Munda Airfields before the invasion of New Georgia on June 30. (Naval History and Heritage Command)

YAMAMOTO'S FINAL OFFENSIVE—THE *I* OPERATION

The Japanese response to the loss of Guadalcanal and reverses on New Guinea was to prepare a large-scale air offensive. This was planned under the personal direction of Yamamoto. The objectives of the operation were to cripple Allied air power, delay the start of the American offensive, and to cover the movement of Japanese ground forces to the Central Solomons. To assemble the weight of air power required for a crippling blow, Yamamoto ordered the Combined Fleet's four carriers in Truk to send their air groups to Rabaul. This resulted in 96 fighters, 65 dive-bombers, and a small number of torpedo bombers heading south. At Rabaul, the carrier air groups joined with the 11th Air Fleet's 86 fighters, 27 dive-bombers, and 72 Betty bombers. The combined total of over 350 aircraft, with the cream of the IJN's air crews, promised decisive results. However, gone were the days when the Japanese could overwhelm Allied defenses by simply massing air power. The Allied defenses on both Guadalcanal and the Papuan Peninsula were much stronger and possessed the invaluable advantage of a fully functioning early warning system which guaranteed any Japanese attack would meet a warm reception.

On April 1, the IJN began the operation with a fighter sweep by 58 Zeros over the Russell Islands. American radar and Allied coastwatchers gave ample warning allowing a mix of 41 Wildcats, Corsairs, and Lightnings to intercept the Japanese force over the Russell Islands. The result was nine Japanese aircraft downed in exchange for nine American aircraft lost.

The first massed air attack of Yamamoto's big offensive was against shipping off Guadalcanal on April 7. Altogether, 157 Zeros and 67 dive-bombers were employed in two waves. In response, the Americans put up 36 F4Fs, nine F4Us, six P-40s, 12 P-38s, and 13 P-39s; of these, 56 made contact with the Japanese. Given advance warning, they were deployed at various altitudes over Savo Island with the P-38s providing top cover. Contact was made at about 1500hrs. While the dogfight raged, the Japanese dive-bombers were able to sink a tanker, the New Zealand corvette *Moa*, and destroyer *Aaron Ward*. The dogfight resulted in seven American fighters and, according to Japanese records, 12 Zeros and nine dive-bombers lost. This one attack satisfied Yamamoto that Allied forces off Guadalcanal had been dealt a severe blow.

The next target on Yamamoto's list was Allied shipping in Oro Bay, New Guinea. On April 11, 72 Zeros escorting 22 dive-bombers hit Allied ships in the bay. The dive-bombers sank a merchantman, damaged another, and damaged an Australian minesweeper. The Zeros were engaged by 50 Allied fighters. Six Zeroes were claimed, and no Allied fighters were lost.

US Navy destroyer *Aaron Ward* on August 17, 1942, photographed during operations in the Solomon Islands area. On top of the foremast is the SC radar, by 1943 she carried the more effective SG. Note the Mk. 4 radar on top of the Mk. 37 Director for her battery of four 5in. guns. She fought in the first naval battle of Guadalcanal on November 13, 1942. Struck by nine shells, she was towed away to fight again. In April 1943, she was sunk by IJN dive-bombers during Yamamoto's Operation *I*. Her wreck was discovered in 1994. (Naval History and Heritage Command)

THE SINKING OF DESTROYER *AARON WARD* (PP. 38–39)

The first massed air attack of Yamamoto's Operation *I* was conducted against shipping off Guadalcanal on April 7. In all, 157 Zeros and 67 dive-bombers were employed in two waves. The first wave was comprised of Zeros and Vals from the 11th Air Fleet and aircraft from carrier *Zuikaku*; the second wave was made up of aircraft from carriers *Hiyo* and *Junyo*. In response, the Americans put up 36 F4Fs, nine F4Us, six P-40s, 12 P-38s, and 13 P-39s; of these, 56 made contact with the Japanese. A massive air battle developed and stretched from the Russell Islands down to Iron Bottom Sound. While the fighters dueled, the Vals made their attacks against the abundance of Allied shipping off Guadalcanal. Dive-bombers from the first wave accounted for the New Zealand corvette *Moa* with two bombs and the tanker *Kanawha* which was hit by two more. The second wave of dive-bombers from *Hiyo*

and *Junyo* focused on the Gleaves-class destroyer *Aaron Ward* **(1)** which was escorting the fully-loaded *LST-449* off Koli Point, Guadalcanal. The destroyer suddenly sighted three Vals coming out of the sun and opened up with her 20mm, 40mm, and 5in. guns and steered hard to port. On this occasion, Japanese dive-bombing were deadly accurate. The first Val scored a near miss **(2)**, which flooded the forward boiler room; the second Val **(3)** placed a direct hit with its 551-pound bomb in the engine room **(4)**; the final aircraft scored another near miss which created additional flooding on the port side aft. A second trio of dive-bombers followed, but none of these scored. The attack killed 20 men, wounded 59, and another seven were missing. The flooding on *Aaron Ward* could not be stopped, and the ship sank that evening.

The following day, 131 Zeros escorted 43 Betty bombers to strike Port Moresby. The Allied were able to get 44 fighters airborne to intercept; the ensuing dogfight resulted in claims for five Japanese fighters for the loss of two Allied aircraft. The level bombers were able to do their work unmolested, but were unable to hit a single ship in the harbor while only damaging a few aircraft at the airfield.

On April 14, Yamamoto mounted his final attack. This time, Milne Bay was selected for attention. A total of 188 aircraft were dispatched to annihilate the shipping reported in the harbor and the aircraft on the nearby airfield. To face this onslaught, only 24 Royal Australian Air Force fighters were able to intercept. Despite excellent bombing conditions, only a single merchantman was lost and two others damaged. Three RAAF aircraft were lost, while claiming seven Japanese.

During the course of these four attacks, Japanese aviators claimed one cruiser, two destroyers, 25 transports, and some 175 Allied aircraft. The real results were much less dramatic—one destroyer, one corvette, one tanker and two merchant ships, and some 25 aircraft. Japanese losses were 61 aircraft—25 Zeros, 21 Vals, and 15 Bettys. Yamamoto was satisfied with the results of the operation and brought the I Operation to an end on April 16. It is unconceivable why Yamamoto thought that only four air attacks would suffice to provide any meaningful results. The operation was undermined by poor target selection, dispersal of effort, and a total failure to follow-up. To provide the desired results, air power must be applied in a concerted manner over time, not in a small number of "decisive" raids as the Japanese preferred. The I Operation was another example of Yamamoto's inability to mass forces on a single objective and it marked the high-water mark for Japanese air power during the Solomons campaign. Even when employed in massed formations, Japanese air power was unable to achieve decisive results. For the remainder of the campaign, the effect of the IJN's land-based air force was gradually decreased. Another indirect consequence of the failure of the I Operation was the death of Yamamoto. On April 18, the G4M bomber he was riding in on an inspection trip to Buin airfield south of Bougainville was shot down by P-38 Lightnings from Guadalcanal.

The I Operation was not the end of Japanese attempts to attack shipping off Guadalcanal. Some of these Japanese incursions were large. On June 7, 81 Zeros headed south to draw Allied fighters into battle. With sufficient warning time from coastwatchers and radar, 104 Allied fighters intercepted and accounted for nine Japanese fighters at the cost of seven American aircraft. Another Japanese fighter sweep on June 12 with 74 Zeros resulted in the loss of seven Zeros and six Allied fighters lost. All this led up to the "Big Raid" on June 16 when the Japanese sent a force of over 100 fighters and bombers to attack shipping off Guadalcanal.

The attack wave was comprised of 70 Zeros escorting 24 dive-bombers. The Allied defense was robust with 74 of 104 intercepting fighters making contact. The Vals were savaged by the defending fighters which accounted for 19 either shot down or damaged. In addition, 15 Zeros were lost and another five damaged. In return, two ships, including one of the first landing ship tanks (LST) in the South Pacific, were forced to beach and only six Allied fighters were lost and two more damaged. This debacle marked the end of daylight Japanese raids over Guadalcanal and showcased the growing impotence of Japanese airpower in the Solomons.

THE INVASION OF NEW GEORGIA

The efforts of IJN land-based aircraft delayed the start of the invasion by about a week. In return, American aircraft operating from Guadalcanal neutralized the Japanese airfields at Munda and Vila. Turner, who had led the invasion of Guadalcanal in August 1942 and then was caught flat-footed by the Japanese response, was determined not to be surprised again. On the night of June 29–30, Rear Admiral Merrill's cruiser-destroyer group conducted a bombardment of the Shortland Islands, the IJN's major naval base in the Solomons. Accompanying minelayers sowed mines in the waters near by. Several support groups from Halsey's Third Fleet, including two carriers, were at sea in case the IJN planned to intervene with forces from Truk.

The American invasion plan called for forces to land at several points to prepare for a direct attack on Munda. Small forces would land at Segi Point, Wickham Anchorage, and Viru Harbor using various minor landing ships and craft. Once secured, these areas would be used to secure the lines of communications to Rendova Island, directly across from Munda, where the main invasion force would land. Following a short build-up period on Rendova, on about D+4, an assault would be made from Rendova across to New Georgia to begin the march on Munda. To cut off Japanese reinforcement of Munda from Kolombangara Island, landings were planned of Enogai Inlet on the Kula Gulf side of New Georgia. Following the seizure of Munda, Vila on the southern tip of Kolombangara was scheduled for attack.

The invasion took the Japanese by surprise. The first indication they had of the operation was when a submarine spotted the US Navy invasion force at midnight on June 29 headed to New Georgia. The Japanese believed that their air offensive had bought them much more time and had failed to stage sufficient air or naval forces to Rabaul to thwart any large-scale invasion.

Turner selected the north coast of Rendova Island just five miles across the Blanche Channel from the airfield at Munda for the main landing. The island was sparsely defended by a force of some 140 Japanese from the 2nd Battalion, 229th Infantry Regiment and a detachment of SNLF troops. The small Japanese garrison offered little opposition and was annihilated by the 172nd Regimental Combat Team (RCT), assisted by local forces. By 1100hrs, the six transports carrying the RCT were half-unloaded. Defended by eight destroyers providing a smoke screen from the Japanese coastal guns against the channel at Munda, the landing had gone according to plan so far.

Japanese air units were also caught by surprise and it was not until 1115hrs that 27 Zeros made a sweep over the beachhead and were treated harshly by American fighters on combat air patrol. Four Zeros were destroyed, and no Allied fighters were lost. This caused a brief delay in unloading, but by 1500hrs the transport force departed the area. Within 30 minutes,

Troops of the 172nd Infantry Regiment take cover on Rendova Island during the initial landings on June 30, 1943. The landing was disorderly, but successful since the Japanese were not expecting a landing on Rendova and resistance was negligible. (Naval History and Heritage Command)

Troops climbing down nets hung over the attack transport USS *McCawley* to board landing craft during rehearsals for the New Georgia operation on June 14, 1943. *McCawley* was a converted passenger line with a fairly high speed of 17 knots. She was Turner's flagship at Guadalcanal, and was sunk on June 30 after the invasion of Rendova while serving in the same capacity. (Naval History and Heritage Command)

they detected incoming Japanese aircraft on radar. This was a force of 24 Zero fighters escorting 25 Betty bombers with torpedoes. Despite an effective interception by a squadron of Marine F4U Corsairs and heavy antiaircraft fire, ten of the torpedo bombers got through to the transports. One placed a torpedo on Turner's flagship *McCawley*; the crew fought a losing battle to save the ship, but the issue was resolved at 2023hrs when two US Navy PT boats took the crippled ship for Japanese and put two more torpedoes into the transport. In exchange for sinking one transport, the IJN lost 19 of 25 Bettys. The final Japanese air attack of the day included 21 Zeros, nine Vals, and 13 F1M floatplanes. No damage was inflicted on any of the American shipping, but one Val and seven of the floatplanes were shot down.

The main landing at Rendova on June 30 was accompanied by others. The southernmost landing was conducted at Wickham Anchorage where a reinforced battalion from the 103rd RCT overcame heavy seas to regroup and attack a Japanese garrison of about 300 men. Within four days the Japanese were annihilated. Segi Point on southern New Georgia was actually occupied by Marine Raiders on June 21 and turned into an emergency airfield following the arrival of construction troops on the 30th. A landing at Viru Harbor by Marine Raiders went awry when the Marines going ashore in rubber boats found the place defended. They landed instead at nearby Segi Point and took the small harbor by overland attack the next day.

The June 30 landings went largely without a hitch against sporadic Japanese opposition. Rendova was the key since it provided a jumping-off point for an attack on Munda and was an ideal location to emplace artillery to support the attack. The

This is the airfield at Segi Point on New Georgia Island. Elements of the 103rd Infantry Regiment were the first to land on New Georgia when they were landed by two destroyer transports at Segi Point on June 21. Improvement of the airfield commenced on June 30 by the 20th Naval Construction Battalion and the field was open for limited operations on July 11. Navy F6F Hellcats used the facility to support the invasion of Bougainville. (Official Marine Corps photo courtesy of Marine Corps History Division)

Fletcher-class destroyer *Strong* highlines mail to cruiser *Honolulu* during operations in early July. Days later, *Strong* was torpedoed and sunk off New Georgia on July 5, 1943 with the loss of 46 men. The torpedo which struck *Strong* came from such a distance that the Americans did not even know they had been engaged by Japanese surface units. (Naval History and Heritage Command)

1st Base Air Force had suffered heavy losses, so the build-up on Rendova was largely undisturbed going forward. A weak attack on July 1 by 34 Zeros and six Vals caused no damage, and saw the loss of another five Zeros and three Vals destroyed. The following day, the IJA and IJN mounted a rare joint strike. Eighteen IJA Ki-21 heavy bombers came in over the beachhead undetected and dropped their ordnance causing 200 casualties. A repeat IJA/IJN performance on July 4 did not go as smoothly. Seventeen Ki-21s, escorted by 17 IJA fighters and 49 Zeros, were intercepted by 32 F4Fs. Six bombers were lost, along with three IJA fighters and a Zero, and damage to targets on the ground was minimal. This marked the end of IJA/IJN joint air operations. The only IJN surface reaction to the invasion was on July 2 when light cruiser *Yubari* and nine destroyers conducted a brief bombardment of the beachhead but hit only adjacent jungle.

The landing on Rendova did concern the IJA enough that it released 4,000 more troops to hold New Georgia. These had to be moved from Rabaul. The only method available was to embark them on destroyers and make a high-speed run at night to Vila. From there, they were moved by barge to New Georgia. This process was scheduled to begin on the night of July 4. Concurrently with this initial movement of Japanese reinforcements, Halsey ordered a landing of three battalions to occupy Rice Anchorage on the northwestern shore of New Georgia to block reinforcements moving from Kolombangara to New Georgia. This was a major operation comprising seven destroyer-transports to carry the 1st Marine Raider Battalion, the 3rd Battalion, 145th Infantry Regiment, and the 3rd Battalion, 148th Infantry Regiment from the 37th Division escorted by Ainsworth's three light cruisers and nine destroyers.

In the first of what would be several actions in these waters, the two forces entered Kula Gulf between New Georgia and Kolombangara. The US Navy was the first to arrive shortly after midnight on July 5. Ainsworth's cruisers and destroyers proceeded to shoot up Vila with some 3,000 6in. shells and a lesser amount of 5in. shells before shifting fire to Bairoko Harbor on New Georgia. Even before the start of the bombardment, a force of four Japanese destroyers, led by the new *Niizuki* which was equipped with one of the first IJN radars, detected Ainsworth's force entering the gulf. The Japanese commander, greatly outnumbered, decided to abort his mission. Before doing so, he ordered 14 torpedoes fired into the gulf before he reversed course and headed north. The retreating Japanese were not detected by American radar until they were almost out of the gulf. Minutes after Ainsworth learned of this contact, a Type 93 torpedo struck the destroyer *Strong* at 0049hrs. Forty-six of her crew were killed and the ship sank at 0124hrs. At no time was the Japanese force taken under fire. Ainsworth did not even think he had been in a surface engagement; he attributed *Strong*'s loss to a submarine torpedo. A torpedo hit from some 22,000 yards was unmatched during the war.

THE BATTLE OF KULA GULF

Halsey had advance notice that the Japanese would try again the following night to reinforce New Georgia. He ordered Ainsworth to return to Kula Gulf and await the Japanese. Ainsworth could muster three light cruisers, *Honolulu*, *Helena*, and *St. Louis*, all Brooklyn-class ships. His screen included four Fletcher-class destroyers *Nicholas*, *O'Bannon*, *Radford*, and *Jenkins*. The last two destroyers were hurriedly rushed from Tulagi to replace the sunken *Strong* and *Chevalier*, which was loaded with the sunken destroyer's survivors. Ainsworth's plan was simple—once radar had detected the Japanese he would use his cruisers to smother them with 6in. fire at the ideal range of 8,000–10,000 yards which he believed was beyond the range of Japanese torpedoes. His destroyers were placed in a subordinate role, using their torpedoes primarily to finish off the Japanese ships crippled by gunfire. This plan has several obvious flaws since it overestimated the capabilities of radar-guided 6in. guns against fast-moving targets, was totally ignorant of the capabilities of the IJN's Type 93 torpedo, and placed the American destroyers in a passive role.

Ainsworth's force arrived off the northwest point of New Georgia at midnight on July 6. His ships were at general quarters and expected trouble. This was on the way in the form of ten IJN destroyers which had departed Buin after sundown and were headed for Vila to land troops and supplies. The force, divided into three sections, was under the command of Rear Admiral Akiyama Teruo. Akiyama was embarked in *Niizuki* and formed his flagship and destroyers *Suzukaze* and *Tanikaze* into a covering force. Three more destroyers, *Mochizuki*, *Mikazuki*, and *Hamakaze* were formed into the First Transport Unit with destroyers *Amagiri*, *Hatsuyuki*, *Nagatsuki*, and *Satsuki* forming the Second Transport Unit. This was not Akiyama's first time as head conductor for a "Tokyo Express" mission, and on this occasion his confidence was bolstered by the presence of radar on *Niizuki* and his large force of ten destroyers.

The largest US Navy ship to be lost in the Solomons campaign was the light cruiser *Helena*. This is a 1943 view of the cruiser. Note that the photo has been censored by the removal of radar from the masts and gun directors, also note the twin 5in. mount abreast the bridge; the last two Brooklyn-class cruisers had their secondary battery placed in twin mounts replacing the single mounts on earlier ships. (Naval History and Heritage Command)

The Naval Battle of Kula Gulf, July 6, 1943

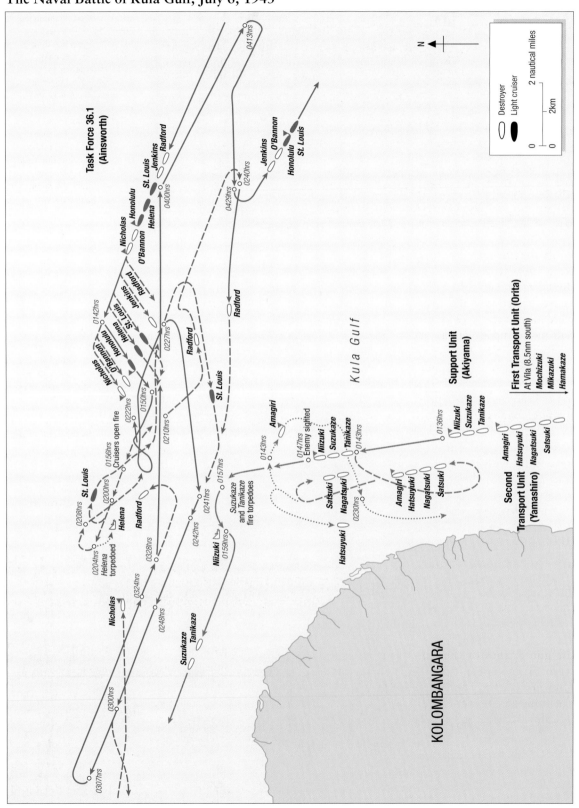

Task Force 36.1 (Ainsworth)

N

Destroyer
Light cruiser

2 nautical miles
2km
0   0

0413hrs

Jenkins
O'Bannon
St. Louis
Honolulu

0440hrs

0429hrs

Radford
Jenkins
St. Louis
Honolulu
Helena

0400hrs

Nicholas
O'Bannon

Radford

0227hrs

Radford

0142hrs

Jenkins
St. Louis
Helena
Honolulu
O'Bannon
Nicholas

0150hrs

0222hrs

St. Louis

Radford

0210hrs

Kula Gulf

Support Unit (Akiyama)

First Transport Unit (Orita)
At Vila (8.5nm south)
Mochizuki
Mikazuki
Hamakaze

Cruisers open fire

0156hrs

0200hrs

St. Louis

0208hrs

0204hrs
Helena torpedoed

Helena

Radford

0328hrs

0241hrs

0242hrs

0157hrs

0136hrs

Niizuki
Suzukaze
Tanikaze

Suzukaze and Tanikaze fire torpedoes

Amagiri

0143hrs

0147hrs
Enemy sighted

Niizuki
Suzukaze
Tanikaze

0143hrs

Satsuki
Nagatsuki

0230hrs

Amagiri
Hatsuyuki
Nagatsuki
Satsuki

Second Transport Unit (Yamashiro)

Amagiri
Hatsuyuki
Nagatsuki
Satsuki

Hatsuyuki

Niizuki

0159hrs

0324hrs

Nicholas

0248hrs

Suzukaze
Tanikaze

0300hrs

0307hrs

KOLOMBANGARA

This is a photograph of an Akizuki-class destroyer taken by Allied aircraft in the South Pacific. This class was just entering service during the Solomons campaign and their large size made them well-suited to act as flagships. *Niizuki* was sunk in this capacity at the Battle of Kula Gulf. Note that the destroyer has only a single torpedo mount, indicating that its primary mission was antiaircraft screening not surface combat. (Naval History and Heritage Command)

By the time Ainsworth's force entered the mouth of the gulf, the Japanese were already inside. By 0143hrs on 6 July, Akiyama had already detached the First Transport Unit and was in the process of detaching the second to deliver its troops and cargo to Vila. He was suspicious that American ships were in the area since as early as 0106hrs the radar detector aboard *Niizuki* had picked up American radar indicating the presence of American ships. At about the time the Second Transport Unit was being detached, American radar came into play picking up the Japanese at 0140hrs at a range of 24,700 yards. The range continued to close with the Japanese headed north in what appeared to be two groups. The cruisers did not receive an order to fire until 0156hrs when the range to Akiyama's covering force was only 7,000 yards. When the first salvos rang out, the range to the lead Japanese ship was a mere 6,800 yards. The Americans had squandered any surprise they may have enjoyed. Just before the first American cruisers opened fire, the three lead Japanese destroyers came to 30 knots and Akiyama recalled the 2nd Transport Group.

The initial American salvos concentrated on *Niizuki* since she was in the lead of the Japanese column and presented the largest radar return. Akiyama's flagship was hit by several 6in. shells, set afire, and later sank; the next two destroyers, *Suzukaze* and *Tanikaze*, suffered only minor damage from the storm of 6in. shells. Their well-drilled torpedo crews quickly put a full salvo of 16 Type 93s headed to where the gun flashes of the American cruisers were easily visible. Since Ainsworth was unaware of the range of the Type 93, by the time he ordered a course change at 0203hrs, it was too late. Three torpedoes struck *Helena*; the cruiser broke in two and the aft section quickly sank. It could have been much worse. Another torpedo hit *St. Louis* but failed to detonate, and another just missed *Honolulu*.

Japanese destroyer *Niizuki* is shown burning at the Battle of Kula Gulf, as seen from the destroyer *Nicholas*. As often happened in night battles, US Navy radar-guided gunfire focused on a single target, allowing the other Japanese ships present to deliver deadly torpedo attacks. *Niizuki* was a big (3,700 tons full load) Akizuki-class destroyer, equipped with radar and had only been commissioned in March. (Naval History and Heritage Command)

Light cruiser *Helena*, in the center of this photograph, is shown firing during the Battle of Kula Gulf. The cruiser firing astern is *St. Louis*. The flashes from the 6in. guns make a fine target, and minutes after this photograph was taken from aboard *Honolulu*, Type 93 torpedoes ravaged *Helena*. (Naval History and Heritage Command)

The next phase of the action featured Ainsworth's two remaining cruisers tracking and then engaging the Second Transport Group. Fire was opened at 11,600 yards at 0218hrs. Of the four destroyers in this group, *Amagiri* escaped with minor damage caused by four 6in. shells; the second ship, *Hatsuyuki* was hit by two 6in. duds and forced out of action; *Nagatsuki* was hit by a single 6in. shell, and the rear ship, *Satsuki*, was undamaged. This marked the essential end of the action other than skirmishes between destroyers on both sides rescuing survivors. The four US Navy destroyers engaged in some futile torpedo attacks, and the cruisers could find no more targets. At 0330hrs, Ainsworth headed back to Tulagi having claimed six IJN ships sunk and several damaged. In fact, the remaining IJN destroyers reached Buin, four by the Blackett Strait and the others by moving along the coast of Kolombangara. *Nagatsuki* ran aground five miles north of Vila and could not be pulled off by *Satsuki*. The stranded ship was attacked by American aircraft the next day and destroyed. The final tally was two IJN destroyers sunk and five damaged. In spite of this, they accomplished their mission, landing 1,600 men and 90 tons of supplies at Vila. In the process, they sank the *Helena* making this a tactical victory for the IJN.

THE BATTLE OF KOLOMBANGARA

In the aftermath of the clash in the Kula Gulf, the Japanese stepped up efforts to reinforce their positions in the Central Solomons. On July 9, Samejima led a force of three cruisers and four destroyers to transport another 1,200 troops to Kolombangara. The mission went off with no opposition from the US Navy. The next run to Kolombangara, scheduled for July 12, would prompt the second major naval clash of the campaign. The Japanese movement on the

The wreck of the Japanese destroyer *Nagatsuki* aground offshore of Kolombangara Island from a photograph taken on May 8, 1944. The destroyer ran aground on July 6 during the Battle of Kula Gulf and was pounded by Allied aircraft later that day. *Nagatsuki* was a member of the 12-ship Mutsuki class; six of them were modified into destroyer transports and were heavily engaged in the Solomons. (Naval History and Heritage Command)

The Naval Battle of Kolombangara, July 12–13, 1943

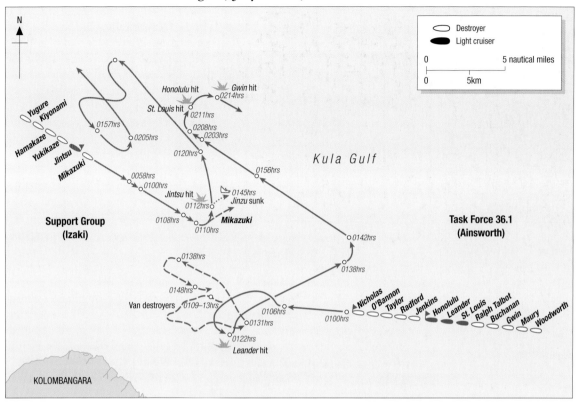

12th was reported by coastwatchers, giving Halsey time to order Ainsworth to head north to stop the IJN from completing its transport mission. For this operation, Ainsworth's force had been augmented and now comprised three light cruisers and ten destroyers. This force was not as strong as those numbers would indicate. Cruisers *Honolulu* and *St. Louis* were joined by the New Zealand light cruiser *Leander*. This ship was in no way comparable to the two US Navy light cruisers since she possessed a top speed of 28 knots (making her the slowest ship in the force) and carried a main battery of only eight slow-firing 6in. guns. The ten destroyers were divided into two sections of five. The first was comprised of five Fletcher-class units, but the second section was a mix from three different destroyer divisions which was added at the last second by Halsey. They had never operated under Ainsworth or worked together before. For this engagement, Ainsworth's plan was the same as the week before at Kula Gulf.

The IJN force at sea for this operation was outnumbered. It was led by Rear Admiral Shunji Izaki on his flagship light cruiser *Jintsu*. Accompanying the cruiser and comprising the covering force were five destroyers. Four more older destroyers embarked the 1,200 troops bound for Kolombangara.

The Battle of Kolombangara was essentially a repeat of the action a week earlier at Kula Gulf. The US Navy had the potential to gain surprise, having received reports at 0035hrs on July 13 of Shunji's approaching force from a PBY scout plane. By 0050hrs, this was converted into a visual contact by one of the lead American destroyers. As the two forces converged, the Japanese commander detached the four ships in the transport group to head to Vila

The Battle of Kolombangara rendered a similar result to the encounter at Kula Gulf. This view shows *St. Louis* and other US Navy ships firing during the battle. The gun flashes provide an obvious target for Japanese torpedo crews. (Naval History and Heritage Command)

and then received word of the approaching US Navy force from a seaplane at 0057hrs. None of the Japanese ships had radar, but their passive radar detectors were able to track the advance of the American force. At 0108hrs, the Japanese gained visual contact.

As usual in a night engagement, the first side to fire invariably gained an advantage. The well-drilled Japanese torpedo crews were off the mark first. Between 0108 and 0114hrs, 22 destroyer torpedoes and seven more from *Jintsu* were on their way south toward the US Navy force. To their credit, three of the five US Navy destroyers in the van of Ainsworth's column also launched a concerted torpedo attack of 19 torpedoes. This attack failed since they were launched at targets 10,000–11,000 yards distant, well beyond the maximum effective range of the Mk. 15 torpedo, and by the fact that the IJN had changed course to the north.

Ainsworth's main punch, his 6in. guns, had yet to make themselves heard. When the Japanese column closed to 10,000 yards, Ainsworth ordered his cruisers to open fire. Moments before, *Jintsu* had used her searchlights to illuminate an American destroyer; this and the fact that she was by far the largest radar return made her the focus of the US Navy barrage which opened at 0112hrs. The two US Navy light cruisers poured out an amazing rate in the next 18 minutes. *Honolulu* fired 1,110 rounds and *St. Louis* another 1,360 6in. rounds joined by a combined 350 5in. rounds. In comparison, *Leander* managed a pathetic 160 6in. rounds. The effect on *Jinstu* was immediate—the first shells to hit the ship struck the rudder, then the bridge was hit killing Izaki, then ten or more shells hit the cruiser's engineering spaces. The doomed and burning *Jintsu* drifted to a stop. The American cruisers assumed *Jintsu* was sunk and shifted fire at 0114hrs to the second target. This target was assumed sunk by 0115hrs, and a third target was engaged.

As the cruisers fired salvo after salvo, the rear group of Ainsworth's destroyers joined the fray. Three destroyers fired some 17 torpedoes, and *Leander* contributed four more commencing at 0114hrs. As the American destroyers were delivering their torpedoes, the initial salvo of Japanese torpedoes arrived in the area of Ainsworth's force. *Leander* was struck by a Type 93 at 0122hrs and crippled.

Leaving two destroyers to stand by *Leander*, Ainsworth assembled his scattered force and headed to the northwest in response to a report from one of *Honolulu*'s aircraft that four Japanese ships were fleeing in that direction. Ainsworth sensed a chance to complete the destruction of the Japanese force. In reality, the Japanese were far from finished. *Jintsu* was out of action and sank spectacularly at 0145hrs after being hit by an American destroyer torpedo. The transport group had completed its mission and was moving north along the coast of Kolombangara. The remaining destroyers of the covering group had reloaded their torpedoes and were heading southeast to re-engage. These were detected by *Honolulu*'s radar at 0156hrs at 20,000 yards range, but by this point the Americans had little situational awareness of where their own forces were. By the time the new contacts were identified

as enemy, the Japanese had fired another barrage of 31 torpedoes. Despite radical maneuvering by Ainsworth, the result was devastating. *St. Louis* was hit by a torpedo and lost her bow. *Honolulu* was also hit by a torpedo forward, and another hit aft but was a dud. Finally, at 0214hrs, destroyer *Gwin* was hit amidships. The only American response during this phase of the battle was a single destroyer firing an ineffectual barrage of four torpedoes at the Japanese.

This brought the battle to an end. The IJN had recorded another resounding victory, though at the cost of *Jintsu* with 482 dead. None of the other IJN ships were even damaged, and the 1,200 troops were delivered to the west coast of Kolombangara safely. The Japanese claimed three Allied cruisers sunk, but all survived. The two American cruisers were back in action by November, but *Leander* was out of action for a year.

ABOVE LEFT
With two torpedo salvos, the Japanese crushed the Allied cruiser force at the Battle of Kolombangara. The first salvo crippled New Zealand Navy light cruiser *Leander*, and the second hit American cruisers *Honolulu* and *St. Louis*. This is a view of the bow of *St. Louis* after the battle. (Naval History and Heritage Command)

ABOVE RIGHT
The second US Navy cruiser crippled at the Battle of Kolombangara was *Honolulu*. This is a view of the cruiser's collapsed bow at Tulagi on July 20, 1943. (Naval History and Heritage Command)

Jinstu was the flagship of Destroyer Squadron 2 and fought in the capacity of a destroyer leader at the Battle of Kolombangara. She was taken under fire early in the battle and crippled by 6in. shellfire; 482 of her crew were killed. This photo shows two of the cruiser's survivors aboard destroyer *Nicholas* after the battle dressed in US Navy working uniforms. (Naval History and Heritage Command)

This photograph shows *Mikasuki* under attack from AAF B-25 bombers on July 28 off Cape Gloucester, New Britain. The ship was sunk, but only eight crewmen were lost. Before her loss, *Mikasuki* participated in the bombardment of Rendova and the Battles of Kula Gulf and Kolombangara. (Naval History and Heritage Command)

Gwin eventually sank with the loss of 61 men dead. For the second time, a US Navy cruiser-destroyer force had been handled roughly by the IJN. After Kolombangara, Nimitz and Halsey realized that using cruisers to chase Japanese destroyers in the restricted waters of the Solomons was not working. From now on, US Navy destroyers would carry the burden alone against the IJN's destroyers reinforcing the various Japanese garrisons.

THE SIEGE OF MUNDA

After a period of build-up and scouting possible landing points, Halsey directed Turner to start his movement to New Georgia. The place selected for the landing was Zanana Beach, about five miles directly east of Munda. The initial movement was made on the afternoon of July 2. Against no opposition, the 1st Battalion, 172nd Infantry Regiment established a perimeter. The remainder of the 172nd Regiment, followed by the 169th Infantry Regiment, was ashore by July 6.

Concurrently with the movement from Rendova, Turner executed a landing at Rice Anchorage on northern New Georgia. Turner decided to land at Rice Anchorage since the Bairoko–Enogai area was strongly held. The operation was delayed by a day, but commencing at 0130hrs on July 5 a mixed force of the 3rd Battalions from the 145th and 148th Infantry Regiments of the 37th Division, joined by the 1st Raider Battalion from Guadalcanal, landed against no opposition.

The American operation had unfolded without major problems and a large force was established on New Georgia. Japanese opposition was thus far ineffective, both on the ground and in the air. This was soon to change when the main body of the Japanese garrison on New Georgia was engaged. On New Georgia and Kolombangara, Sasaki had some 10,500 men, primarily deployed to guard Munda. Clashes with the Americans in the area of Zanana occurred on July 3, and the following day Sasaki moved the 3rd Battalion of the 229th Infantry Regiment from Vila over to Munda. Sasaki's strength increased further following the arrival of 850 men after the Battle of Kula Gulf, and he moved another battalion to Munda from Kolombangara.

The 6th Kure SNLF was positioned to defend Bairoko Harbor, the New Georgia terminus of the Japanese supply line from Kolombangara. The three battalions of the American Northern Landing Force began to move on Bairoko on July 5. Over difficult terrain, they covered some five miles on the first day without meeting any opposition. It took until July 11 until the Marine Raiders cleared a small force from the 6th Kure SNLF from Enogai Point and captured the four 140mm costal guns emplaced there. The 3rd Battalion, 148th Infantry Regiment held a blocking position on an inland trail from July 8 to 17. The Americans believed this was a key position since it supposedly blocked Munda from receiving reinforcements from Bairoko. This was not the case. The Japanese 13th Infantry Regiment was able to join the garrison at Munda and the 2nd Battalion, 45th Infantry Regiment was

The 1st Marine Raider Battalion was assigned the mission of capturing Enogai Point and Bairoko Harbor to cut of the flow of Japanese reinforcements from Kolombangara. This photo shows Marines near Enogai Point. The very difficult terrain, as evident in the photo, combined with supply problems and lack of firepower, meant that movement of Japanese reinforcements to Munda was never curtailed. (Official Marine Corps photo courtesy of Marine Corps History Division)

committed from Vila to reinforce the defenses at Bairoko. The American attempt to cut-off Munda from reinforcement had failed.

The main American attack from Zanana to Munda Airfield was slow to develop and quickly ran into trouble. American planners underestimated the terrain along the coast. The terrain was not just covered by jungle, it was also swampy, crossed by streams, and most challengingly covered by rocky hills up to 300ft high. There was no road, only a single trail able to take only foot traffic. On July 4, Hester began a two-regiment attack toward the Barike River some three miles distant. By July 6, the 172nd Regiment reached the river, but the 169th Infantry Regiment, advancing inland, ran into 11th Company, 229th Infantry Regiment and took until July 8 to reach its objective. With both regiments in place, Hester ordered a general attack toward Munda on the 9th.

The attack kicked off at 0500hrs on July 9. It was preceded by 5,800 artillery shells, including by 155mm weapons firing from Rendova, another 2,344 5in. shells from four destroyers, and 70 tons of bombs from 88 aircraft. The attack was a bust, even in the face of limited opposition. The bad terrain limited the 172nd Infantry Regiment to 1,100 yards gain; the 169th Infantry Regiment gained nothing. It was a bad omen for things to come. The inexperienced American troops, particularly the shaken 169th Infantry Regiment, performed very poorly. The attack resumed the following day, and proved more successful, but the main Japanese defense had not been encountered.

On the 11th, the 169th Infantry Regiment continued along the Munda trail. Hester ordered the 172nd Infantry Regiment to disengage and move to the south to reach Laiana and advance on Munda from there. It took until July 13 for the 172nd Infantry Regiment to reach Laiana struggling through the swamp without resupply. Once there, it was reinforced by the 3rd Battalion, 103rd Infantry Regiment and a platoon of Marine light tanks.

By the 15th, the Americans had made only tactical progress. Both regiments were now in contact with the main Japanese defense line and the 169th Infantry Regiment had gained some important high ground. However,

the cost had been high. Combat casualties were limited to 90 killed and 636 wounded, but disease accounted for over 1,000 men and a serious problem with combat fatigue was emerging. Leadership in the 43rd Division had been found wanting. Hester relieved the commander of the 169th Infantry Regiment and one of the regiment's battalion commanders. The larger issue of command was addressed when Harmon convinced Halsey to insert Griswold as commander of the New Georgia Occupation Force. Griswold arrived on July 11; Hester reverted to command of the 43rd Division. Griswold took immediate stock of the situation, informing Harmon that the 43rd Division was on the verge of collapse and that the remainder of the 37th Division and the 25th Division were needed to complete the capture of Munda.

THE AMERICANS REGROUP

Griswold assumed command at midnight on July 15. This was his first combat experience. He decided to suspend the attack on Munda in order to straighten out his supply problems and prepare a full corps attack. In response to his request for more troops, the 145th Regiment of the 37th Division and the 161st RCT from the 25th Division were sent forward from Guadalcanal. While the build-up continued, the Americans launched only local attacks on the Munda front from July 16 to 24.

While the Americans struggled forward, the aggressive Sasaki prepared to counterattack. He received permission to bring the entire 13th Infantry Regiment over from Kolombangara. With its 1st and 3rd Battalions, Sasaki believed he had a force large enough to bring decisive results. He planned to employ this regiment to strike the exposed right flank of the 169th Infantry Regiment and encircle and destroy the Americans on New Georgia. In fact, the 43rd Division was vulnerable with its right flank open and its lines of communication back to Zanana exposed. On the night of July 14, the counterattack began with six infantry companies. Movement was extremely difficult in the impossible terrain and it was not until the night of the 17th that the Japanese fell upon the rear areas of the 43rd Division. The 43rd Division's command post was attacked, but the Japanese were repelled with heavy losses by well-directed artillery. Some Japanese made it as far as Zanana, but a scratch American force repulsed that attack as well. Much remains unclear about the movements of the Japanese force since records are skimpy, but what is certain is that American lines of communications were not disrupted. A supporting attack by the 229th Infantry Regiment was also unsuccessful. The 229th Infantry Regiment's 3rd Battalion attacked along the high ground against the 1st Battalion from the 169th Infantry Regiment and was contained after making some initial progress. The 229th Infantry Battalion's 2nd Battalion attacked the 3rd Battalion, 103rd Infantry Regiment but was easily repulsed. Sasaki's counterattack was a total failure, primarily because the Japanese commander had failed to account for the effects of terrain.

While the Japanese counterattack was faltering in the jungle, the Americans suffered similar problems in the area of Bairoko where the Japanese were defending with the 2nd Battalion, 13th Infantry Regiment and elements of the Kure 6th SNLF. The 2nd Battalion, 45th Infantry Regiment reinforced the defenders on the night of July 12–13. On July 18, the 4th Marine Raider Battalion joined the 1st Raider Battalion and prepared to renew the attack with the two Army battalions still in place. Since the Raider battalions were under strength, the entire American force was without artillery, and air support proved difficult to coordinate, the renewed attack on July 20 stalled after some initial progress. Bairoko harbor remained in Japanese hands and the Northern Landing Force was spent.

THE FINAL ATTACK ON MUNDA

By July 24, XIV Corps was ready to commence its attack. The 37th Division was deployed inland with the 145th Infantry Regiment farthest south, the 161st Infantry Regiment in the center, and the 148th Infantry Regiment in the north providing flank protection. The 43rd Division remained along the coast with the 172nd and 103rd Infantry Regiments on line. The 169th Infantry Regiment had been relieved and was sent to corps reserve. A total of 12 infantry battalions were ready for the attack. Opposing them were the three depleted battalions of the 229th Infantry Regiment and a company from the 230th Infantry Regiment. The Japanese defense was bolstered by a number of antitank and antiaircraft units, with the 13th Infantry Regiment in reserve. Sasaki still intended to use it to strike the Americans' right flank.

A typical Japanese bunker on New Georgia was made from coconut logs and coral. They were 10–12 feet square and had three or four layers of logs banked with 6–8 feet of coral. Only the top 2–3 feet remained above ground. Each had firing slits for riflemen and a heavy machine gun. The bunkers were so well camouflaged that only after they opened fire was it possible to spot the position. This is how the Japanese garrison brought the American advance to Munda to a crawl while withstanding constant bombardment from artillery and aircraft. (Official Marine Corps photo courtesy of Marine Corps History Division)

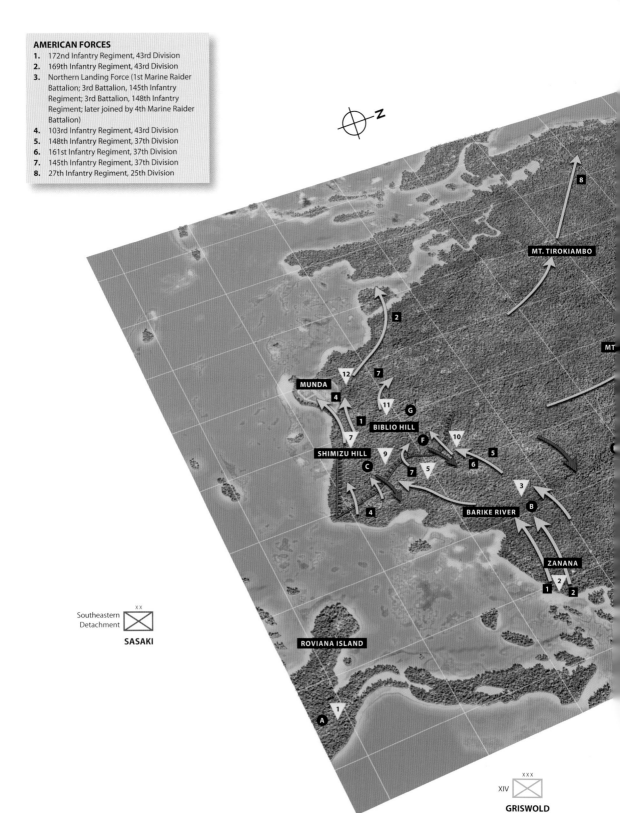

AMERICAN FORCES
1. 172nd Infantry Regiment, 43rd Division
2. 169th Infantry Regiment, 43rd Division
3. Northern Landing Force (1st Marine Raider Battalion; 3rd Battalion, 145th Infantry Regiment; 3rd Battalion, 148th Infantry Regiment; later joined by 4th Marine Raider Battalion)
4. 103rd Infantry Regiment, 43rd Division
5. 148th Infantry Regiment, 37th Division
6. 161st Infantry Regiment, 37th Division
7. 145th Infantry Regiment, 37th Division
8. 27th Infantry Regiment, 25th Division

MT. TIROKIAMBO

MT

MUNDA

BIBLIO HILL

SHIMIZU HILL

BARIKE RIVER

ZANANA

Southeastern Detachment

SASAKI

ROVIANA ISLAND

XIV

GRISWOLD

THE BATTLE FOR NEW GEORGIA ISLAND, JUNE 30–AUGUST 5

The slow American advance to take the airfield

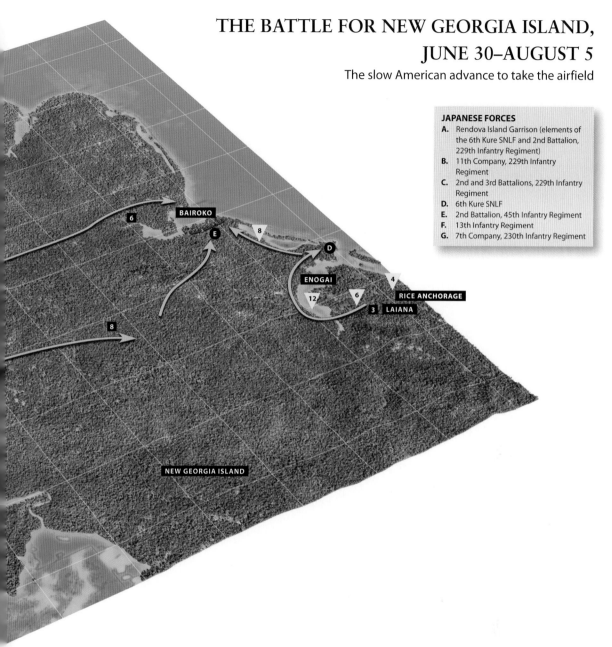

JAPANESE FORCES
- **A.** Rendova Island Garrison (elements of the 6th Kure SNLF and 2nd Battalion, 229th Infantry Regiment)
- **B.** 11th Company, 229th Infantry Regiment
- **C.** 2nd and 3rd Battalions, 229th Infantry Regiment
- **D.** 6th Kure SNLF
- **E.** 2nd Battalion, 45th Infantry Regiment
- **F.** 13th Infantry Regiment
- **G.** 7th Company, 230th Infantry Regiment

BAIROKO

ENOGAI

RICE ANCHORAGE

LAIANA

NEW GEORGIA ISLAND

▼ EVENTS

1. June 30: the 172nd Infantry Regiment lands on Rendova Island and overwhelms the small Japanese garrison.

2. July 2: 1st Battalion, 172nd Infantry Regiment lands on New Georgia Island against no opposition; the remainder of the 172nd Infantry Regiment and the entire 169th Infantry Regiment are ashore by 6 July.

3. July 4: the 169th and 172nd Infantry Regiments attack toward Munda. The advance is slowed by extremely rugged terrain and a company from the 229th Infantry Regiment; the Barike River is reached by July 8.

4. July 5: the Northern Landing Force lands at Rice Anchorage against no opposition.

5. July 9: the169th and 172nd Infantry Regiments resume the attack toward Munda with intense air, artillery and naval gunfire support. Against the terrain and the Japanese 229th Infantry Regiment, it takes until the 15th to reach the main Japanese defenses.

6. July 11: the Northern Landing Force clears Enogai but is unable to reach Bairoko; Japanese defenses are reinforced by the 2nd Battalion, 45th Infantry Regiment.

7. July 14: Sasaki launches a counterattack, but the advance of the 13th Infantry Regiment is stilted by impossible terrain. By the 17th, two battalions of the regiment launch small-scale attacks against the rear of the 43rd Division but are repulsed. The 2nd and 3rd Battalions of the 229th Infantry Regiment launch a supporting attack but are also repulsed.

8. July 18–20: the Northern Landing Force, reinforced by the 4th Marine Raider Battalion, resumes its attack to Bairoko, but is unable to reach the harbor.

9. July 25: Griswold begins a corps-level attack with 12 infantry battalions and intensive air, artillery and naval gunfire support. Initial progress is slow, but Japanese casualties continue to mount.

10. July 28: the Japanese 13th Infantry Regiment launches a counterattack at the seam of the 148th and 161st Infantry Regiments; the Americans are forced to conduct a tactical retreat, but their overall advance is not stopped.

11. July 30: with his defenses about to break, Sasaki orders a retreat.

12. August 5: XIV Corps occupies Munda with little opposition. Japanese forces retreat north to Bairoko and west to Baanga Island.

XIV CORPS ATTACKS SHIMIZU HILL (PP. 58–59)

On July 25, the American XIV Corps launched the biggest attack of the campaign to break through Japanese defenses in front of Munda Airfield. The 43rd Division was on the American left flank and it attacked with three regiments abreast. After the artillery lifted at 0700hrs, the infantry moved forward. In the sector of the 172nd Infantry Regiment, the attack of the regiment's 2nd and 3rd Battalions was supported by five Marine M3 light tanks **(1)**. The objective was to seize Shimizu Hill, which was only some 1,000 yards from the edge of the airfield. This scene depicts the combined tank-infantry assault **(2)** on the dug-in Japanese defenders from the 2nd Battalion, 229th Infantry Regiment. With its large trees on the crest, the hill could not be surmounted by the M3s. Japanese defenders firing from bunkers picked off the infantry, and when three of the tanks stopped cold from vapor lock, the attack faltered. It took until August 5 to cross the last 1,000 yards to the airfield.

When the American attack began on the 25th, it was preceded by an extensive firepower preparation. Seven destroyers pumped 5in. rounds into the Japanese positions, over 3,300 artillery rounds were fired, and 254 aircraft added to the chaos. In spite of this weight of firepower, initial results were disappointing. The 37th Division made no progress and the 43rd Division made only small gains in the center. The following day, the Americans made their first use of flame throwers and with Marine light tanks began to make progress. On a front of only 600 yards, the 103rd Infantry Regiment encountered 74 pillboxes. The Americans continued to grind away from July 28 to 31, and took

In this photo, a Marine inspects the interior of a Japanese coconut-log bunker in the Munda area after its capture. The well-built nature of the position is evident. (Official Marine Corps photo courtesy of Marine Corps History Division)

Shimizu Hill, the last ridge before the airfield. To maintain the advance, two battalions of the 169th Infantry Regiment were committed. On July 28, the Japanese 13th Infantry Regiment attacked the 148th Infantry Regiment and exploited gaps with the neighboring 161st RCT. The 148th was forced to retreat to secure a continuous line.

The weight of American firepower and the constant pressure from two divisions began to tell. Sasaki informed Samejima that his lines were about to crumble. The 229th Infantry Regiment was down to 1,245 men. After conferring with an 8th Fleet staff officer sent from Rabaul on the 30th, Sasaki ordered a retreat to a position north of the airfield.

When the Americans attacked on August 1, the 43rd Division made rapid progress. It became apparent the Japanese main force had withdrawn. The 103rd Infantry Regiment reached the edge of the airfield, and the 27th Infantry Regiment of the 25th Infantry Division arrived to spearhead the

Munda Airfield shown after its capture; work to refurbish the airfield has already begun. The first aircraft to use the facility touched down on September 24. Munda was the most important airfield used to support the Bougainville invasion since it was the base for over 100 Navy and Marine Dauntless and Avenger aircraft, as well as Navy Corsairs and AAF P-39s. (Official Marine Corps photo courtesy of Marine Corps History Division)

Even after the capture of Munda Airfield, the Japanese attempted to hold neighboring Baanga and Arundel Islands as a possible launching point for a future counterattack. Arundel was not captured until September 21 when the Japanese garrison was evacuated to Kolombangara Island. This is a Japanese bunker on Baanga Island. (Official Marine Corps photo courtesy of Marine Corps History Division)

advance which was now becoming a pursuit. Led by the tank platoons of the 9th and 10th Marine Defense Battalions, the airfield was secured on the afternoon of August 5.

Sasaki decided that New Georgia couldn't be defended the day before the airfield finally fell to the Americans. Accordingly, the 13th Regiment was ordered to Kolombangara, along with the remnants of the 6th SNLF. The remaining forces on New Georgia, the 229th Regiment, the 2nd Battalion of the 230th Infantry Regiment, and the 3rd Battalion of the 23rd Infantry Regiment, were moved to Baanga Island, some 4,000 yards west of Munda. Sasaki hoped to maintain forces on Baanga in the hopes that additional forces would be forthcoming from Rabaul for a counterattack.

As the Japanese defense dissolved, the fresh 27th Infantry Regiment was assigned to lead the drive to Bairoko and to the northwest to cut off the retreating Japanese. Advancing through trackless terrain, which was much more of an obstacle than the retreating Japanese, the village of Zieta on the northwest part of New Georgia was taken on August 15. Bairoko finally fell on August 25.

Sasaki's plan to hold Baanga was short lived. The 43rd Division was assigned to capture it, beginning on August 11. By this time, and in the aftermath of the naval defeat at Vella Gulf when a battalion from the 6th Division was lost, the 8th Fleet ordered a retreat from Baanga to Arundel Island. By August 22, Baanga was evacuated.

INVASION OF VELLA LAVELLA

The capture of New Georgia made Vila on Kolombangara Halsey's next target. Sasaki expected the next American attack to hit Vila and had prepared heavy defenses on the southern part of Kolombangara Island. Halsey wanted no repeat of the slugfest at Munda. The solution was to bypass heavily defended Kolombangara and land on undefended Vella Lavella 35nm northwest of Munda. This had the key attribute of avoiding the teeth of the Japanese defenses and was easily covered by aircraft flying out of Munda which opened for flight operations on August 14.

The landing on August 15 was unopposed. The assault force included the 35th RCT from the 25th Infantry Division and the 4th Marine Defense Battalion. The only Japanese on the island were 250 stragglers from the Vella Gulf naval battle. This was Wilkinson's first landing operation, and he planned to unload the transports in 12 hours before the Japanese could respond.

The Japanese air reaction was light. The invasion force was spotted by a Japanese aircraft at 0300hrs, but the first air attack by a mere six dive-bombers escorted by 48 fighters did not arrive until 0800hrs. No ships were hit, but some casualties were suffered to strafing. Just after noon, another 11 dive-bombers and 48 fighters made an appearance, attacking some LSTs and causing no damage. The final wave of the day (eight dive-bombers and 32 fighters) arrived at about 1730hrs and again caused no damage. Defending American fighters claimed 17 attackers from the last two waves. The landing was a complete success. For only 12 dead and 40 wounded to air attack, the Americans put a force of some 6,000 troops on Vella Lavella and completely unhinged the Japanese defense of the Central Solomons.

THE NAVAL BATTLE OF VELLA GULF

The close of the battle for New Georgia and the landing on Vella Lavella brought a spike in naval operations. In the aftermath of their victory at Kolombangara on July 13, the Japanese conducted another reinforcement effort on July 19 supported by three heavy cruisers. This was an attempt to inflict a sharp defeat on any intervening US Navy force, but instead the operation resulted in damage to heavy cruiser *Suzuya* and another destroyer, and two more destroyers sunk by air attack. After this minor fiasco, the Japanese decided that the direct route to Vila was too risky. Two runs on July 22 and August 1 were successfully conducted through the Vella Gulf on the western side of Kolombangara. It was during the August 1 operation that a Japanese destroyer rammed and sank US Navy *PT 109* which was commanded by future American president John Kennedy. The Japanese planned a repeat performance on August 6.

This next operation would be opposed by the US Navy, and by an American force under new leadership using more aggressive tactics. Wilkinson encouraged new ideas and new tactics. Among his new destroyer squadron commanders were Commanders Arleigh Burke, Frederick Moosbrugger, and Rodger Simpson. Burke was not present at the next clash, but Moosbrugger and Simpson built a battle plan on a radar-guided night torpedo attack. After gaining radar contact with the enemy, Moosbrugger's force of three destroyers would launch torpedoes

This is the Mahan-class destroyer *Dunlop* photographed in May 1942. In August 1943, she was Commander Moosbrugger's flagship at the Battle of Vella Gulf. She took part in the initial torpedo strike of 22 torpedoes which crippled or sank three of four IJN destroyers present. (Naval History and Heritage Command)

The Naval Battle of Vella Gulf, August 6–7, 1943

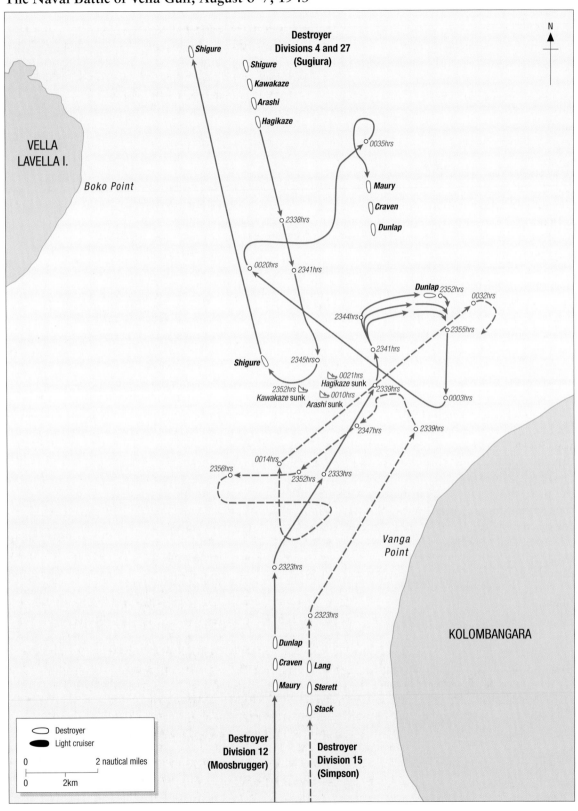

N

VELLA
LAVELLA I.

Boko Point

**Destroyer
Divisions 4 and 27
(Sugiura)**

Shigure

Shigure

Kawakaze

Arashi

Hagikaze

0035hrs

Maury

Craven

Dunlap

2338hrs

0020hrs

2341hrs

Dunlap 2352hrs

0032hrs

2344hrs

2355hrs

2341hrs

Shigure

2345hrs

0003hrs

2352hrs

Kawakaze sunk

0021hrs

Hagikaze sunk

0010hrs

Arashi sunk

2339hrs

2347hrs

2339hrs

2356hrs

0014hrs

2352hrs

2333hrs

Vanga
Point

2323hrs

KOLOMBANGARA

2323hrs

Dunlap

Craven

Maury

Lang

Sterett

Stack

Destroyer   Destroyer
Light cruiser

0   2 nautical miles

0   2km

**Destroyer
Division 12
(Moosbrugger)**

**Destroyer
Division 15
(Simpson)**

while Simpson's three destroyers would engage with gunfire after the torpedoes struck. This was the first time in the Solomons campaign that the US Navy planned to use the torpedo as its primary offensive weapon. Combined with radar and favorable tactical circumstances, it was a plan for a resounding victory.

The Japanese were repeating the same plan which had worked in earlier runs. A force of four destroyers were ordered to approach Kolombangara from the west, entering Vella Gulf and moving into the Blackett Strait where troops and supplies would be loaded into barges for final movement to Vila. The Japanese force was under the overall command of Captain Sugiura Kaju with Captain Hara Tameichi in command of a single destroyer. Hara was an outspoken critic of what he saw as the IJN's sloppy planning and is well known to English-speaking audiences since his post-war book about his wartime experiences was translated into English. In a pre-departure conference, Hara warned his fellow commanders that repeating the operation was courting disaster.

Both sides entered Vella Gulf late on August 6. Both sides expected a clash since an American reconnaissance aircraft had spotted the approaching Japanese force earlier in the day. Sugiura knew that he had lost the element of surprise and assumed that a night engagement was possible. His force entered Vella Gulf from the north with his flagship *Hagikaze* in the lead of a compact column. American forces entered the gulf from the south in two columns with Moosbrugger's ships in the lead. It was a very dark night with no moon, favoring the Americans.

Moosbrugger's ships gained a major advantage when at 2333hrs the radar on his flagship *Dunlap* gained contact on the Japanese at a range of 19,700 yards. Japanese lookouts failed on this occasion, probably because of the lack of moonlight and by the fact that Kolombangara Island was behind the Americans, allowing them to blend into the darkness. The result was disaster. Moosbrugger began to line-up torpedo attacks on the oblivious Japanese, which radar soon defined as four separate contacts.

The Japanese closed to within 6,300 yards before Moosbrugger ordered his three destroyers to launch torpedoes. At 2341hrs, 22 torpedoes left their mounts for their short run to the still oblivious Japanese destroyers. Immediately after launching his torpedo barrage, Moosbrugger turned his ships away to present as small a target as possible against a potential Japanese response. At the last second, Japanese lookouts spotted the American destroyers against Kolombangara, followed by torpedo wakes.

It was too late to take evasive measures. Beginning at 2345hrs, at least five of the 22 torpedoes hit their targets. *Hagikaze* was struck by two torpedoes, and the second hit aft in the engine room which brought her to a stop. *Arashi*, next in column, was also hit by two torpedoes which destroyed her machinery spaces. Next to be hit was *Kawakaze* which was struck by a single torpedo under the bridge which detonated the forward magazine and set the ship afire. Hara's *Shigure*, the last ship in column, had a miraculous escape. After sighting the torpedoes, Hara's well-trained crew got a full eight-torpedo broadside off against the Americans. None of these hit a target. Two American torpedoes came within some 20 yards of *Shigure* and another went through the ship's rudder without exploding.

The rest of the battle was spent mopping up the three crippled IJN destroyers. At 2347hrs, Simpson's ships engaged *Kawakaze*, now only some 3,000 yards to the northwest, with their 5in. guns. Hit by this intense gunfire, and possibly by some of the four torpedoes launched at her, *Kawakaze* sank at 2352hrs. *Arashi* and *Hagikaze* fired back ineffectively with their 5in. guns, and soon all six American destroyers were concentrating their fire on the two burning Japanese ships. *Arashi*'s magazine blew up at 0100hrs. *Hagikaze* was the target of another six torpedoes launched at 0021hrs; three were heard to explode causing *Hagikaze* to disappear.

Hara decided to take *Shigure* back to Rabaul, bringing the action to a close. For the first time in the war, IJN destroyers had been beaten in a night action. In addition to the three ships lost, of the approximately 1,520 Japanese sailors and soldiers that went into the waters off Vella Lavella, only 310 survived.

THE BATTLE OFF HORANIU

The American decision to bypass Kolombangara brought on the next naval action. The Japanese response was to land troops at Horaniu on the northeastern part of Vella Lavella Island to build a barge base to maintain a line of communication with the garrison on Kolombangara. Accordingly, on August 17, a force of four IJN destroyers under the command of Rear Admiral Ijuin Matsuji departed Rabaul. These were assigned to escort a flotilla of 22 small craft bringing the troops to Horaniu. The small craft also departed on August 17 from Buin south of Bougainville. They were quickly spotted by Allied air reconnaissance and a division of four destroyers under Captain T. J. Ryan was ordered to intercept.

Both commanders knew that they were likely to face opposition, but the resulting action was indecisive and the Japanese garrison bound for Horaniu arrived safely. The action began at 0027hrs on August 18 when the radar aboard *O'Bannon* reported the IJN force to the northwest at 23,000 yards range. Minutes later at 0032hrs, lookouts aboard *Sazanami* spotted the US Navy destroyers at a range of 16,400 yards to the southeast. Neither side had gained the advantage of surprise.

Ijuin was restricted tactically since his primary mission was to get the convoy through to Horaniu, not engage the Americans. When both sides gained contact, the convoy was still some 16 miles short of its destination and was located between the opposing destroyer forces. Ijuin ordered two of his destroyers to the north to draw the Americans away from the convoy; his flagship *Sazanami* and *Hamakaze* remained near the convoy to provide protection. The American commander Ryan wanted to repeat the winning formula from Vella Gulf and maneuvered his force for a

Fletcher-class destroyer *Nicholas* firing her forward 5in./38 guns at Japanese destroyers during the Battle off Horaniu. During this inconclusive battle, the four US Navy destroyers present fired 3,028 5in. shells and inflicted only light damage on two Japanese destroyers. Even with radar, it was extremely difficult to hit a fast, maneuvering target. (Naval History and Heritage Command)

surprise torpedo attack. This plan was thwarted when a Japanese floatplane dropped a flare over the American force at 0040hrs. Ryan then turned to engage the convoy which was located to his east.

In response to the American threat to the convoy, Ijuin ordered a massive torpedo attack. Beginning at 0046hrs, his four destroyers launched a total of 31 torpedoes at Ryan's force from a range of approximately 12,500 yards. On several previous occasions, this would have been enough to bring success, but Ryan unintentionally ordered two turns between 0050–0054hrs which placed his force out of harm. The Japanese followed their unsuccessful torpedo attack with a gunnery attack. Though the American destroyers were silhouetted in front of a full moon, IJN gunnery was ineffective since they were unwilling to use searchlights for fear of revealing their position. Again, no US Navy ships were hit.

Ryan temporarily abandoned his barge hunt and headed north after the Japanese destroyers. His ships opened a barrage of radar-guided 5in. gunnery at the Japanese. The Americans straddled their targets, but only inflicted minor damage to *Hamakaze* and *Isokaze*. *Chevalier* had launched four torpedoes at a range of 9,000 yards with no effect; *Shigure* and *Isokaze* fired additional torpedoes, but again with no effect. When Ijuin received a report of a large enemy force nearby from *Hamakaze*, he broke off the action. Ryan declined to pursue and returned to the location of the convoy now to his southeast. The Japanese small craft had scattered during the destroyer action, and the Americans were only able to locate and destroy a single barge and two submarine chasers. The rest of the convoy reached the relative safety of the coast of Vella Lavella Island and arrived at Horaniu the next night.

THE JAPANESE RETREAT FROM THE CENTRAL SOLOMONS

After the American landing on Vella Lavella, there was no major ground combat on the island. The Japanese garrison force totaled some 390 men in two rifle companies and a platoon of SNLF, which arrived by August 19. The Japanese continued to contest the build-up of American forces on the island with air attacks. The second echelon of the invasion was attacked by Japanese aircraft on August 16 and lost an LST. The third echelon was attacked on August 21 and suffered no damage.

After completing their build-up, the American forces on Vella Lavella began to advance along both coasts. One battalion was ordered to clear Kokolope Bay where the Japanese barge base was located. The Japanese did not contest the advance, and Horaniu was captured on September 14. On September 18, the 14th New Zealand Brigade Group landed on Vella Lavella to complete the capture of the island. The small Japanese garrison escaped, but the Americans were able to get a new airfield on the island operational by September 24.

Much more severe combat was taking place on Arundel Island, located between New Georgia and Kolombangara Islands. The Americans landed on August 27, were eventually forced to commit eight infantry battalions, and the island was not cleared until September 21. The battle only came to an end when Sasaki was ordered to retreat. The order was part of Imperial General Headquarters' new strategy to hold the Central Solomons only

The 14th New Zealand Brigade Group (similar in size and capabilities to a US Army regimental combat team), is shown here landing on Vella Lavella Island on September 18. The New Zealanders were assigned to finish securing the island, but the small Japanese garrison escaped. (Official Marine Corps photo courtesy of Marine Corps History Division)

A Japanese *"daihatsu"* landing craft swamped on a New Georgia beach in July 1943. These craft proved supremely useful during the Solomons campaign. They could carry 70 men or 10 tons of cargo at a speed of about 8 knots. They were armed with up to a 37mm gun and were armored to defeat light weapons. Moving at night and camouflaged during the day, they were tough to find and more difficult to sink. They were the prime reason the Japanese were able to supply and then evacuate their Central Solomons garrison. (Official Marine Corps photo courtesy of Marine Corps History Division)

until late September–early October to allow time to strengthen defenses on Bougainville. When Sasaki was informed of the new strategy on September 15, he prepared to move his approximately 12,435 men, mainly on Kolombangara, by barge and destroyer. These barges, or *daihatsu*, had proved very effective since they were hard to spot and sink by aircraft, too small to hit effectively with destroyers, and were able to contend with American PT boat attacks.

The evacuation was well-planned by Samejima and his staff and featured excellent IJA and IJN cooperation. It began on the night of September 28–29 and concluded on the night of October 2–3. The exact numbers of men evacuated is hard to determine, but by combined efforts of barges and destroyers, the total may have been as high as 9,400. In any event, it was many more then the Japanese expected to rescue. The US Navy attempted

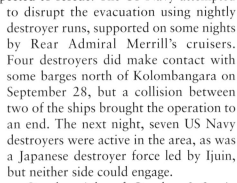

to disrupt the evacuation using nightly destroyer runs, supported on some nights by Rear Admiral Merrill's cruisers. Four destroyers did make contact with some barges north of Kolombangara on September 28, but a collision between two of the ships brought the operation to an end. The next night, seven US Navy destroyers were active in the area, as was a Japanese destroyer force led by Ijuin, but neither side could engage.

On the night of October 2–3, six American destroyers were ordered to the area off Kolombangara. Ijuin was also at sea with nine destroyers. The four Japanese destroyers ordered to pick up troops on Kolombangara were subjected to two ineffectual torpedo attacks. This was followed by a general gunnery duel between the two forces at 8,000 yards range which only resulted in three dud 5in. shells striking *Shigure*. A Japanese barrage of 14 Type 93s was also ineffective. On the final night of the evacuation, the Americans only netted five barges. Despite claims of sinking 46 barges and therefore killing thousands of Japanese, the US Navy's efforts to stop the Japanese retreat from Kolombangara were unsuccessful. Many of the veteran troops would be encountered again on Bougainville.

THE NAVAL BATTLE OF VELLA LAVELLA

The next naval clash was prompted by a Japanese evacuation of the 590 men left on Vella Lavella. Rear Admiral Ijuin was given this responsibility. He formed a covering group of six destroyers to protect a transport group of three destroyers and 12 smaller craft. As soon as Ijuin's force left Rabaul on October 6, it was spotted by American aircraft. In response, six US Navy destroyers were ordered to intercept, but only three under the command of Captain Frank Walker were involved in the action.

First contact was made by American radar of Ijuin's six covering destroyers at 2231hrs. Japanese lookouts spotted the American force within minutes after the Americans gained radar contact. They reported four ships which correlated nicely to a report from a Japanese aircraft of one cruiser and three destroyers being present. Both sides were determined to engage. Walker's determination was remarkable since he knew as many as nine IJN destroyers could be in the area. Both sides continued to close, and both planned torpedo attacks. Ijuin missed the chance to employ his long-range Type 93s, and then proceeded to execute a maneuver which silhouetted his

The Battle of Vella Lavella on October 6 resulted in a split decision. Both sides lost a destroyer, but the Japanese missed a chance to inflict a more severe reverse on the US Navy. This view shows the damaged *Selfridge* which took a torpedo on her bow. The destroyer moored alongside is *O'Bannon*, which collided with *Chevalier* which later sank. (Naval History and Heritage Command)

The Naval Battle of Vella Lavella, October 6–7, 1943

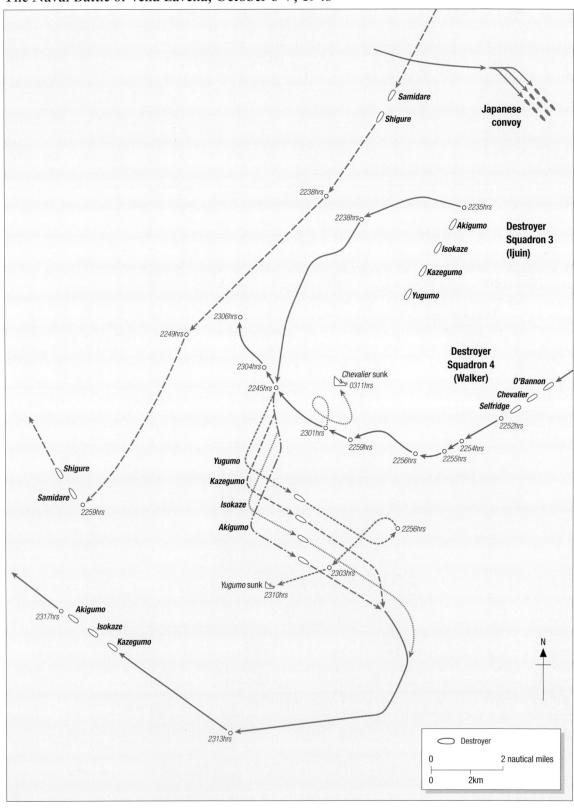

Samidare

Shigure

Japanese convoy

2238hrs

2238hrs

2235hrs

Akigumo

Isokaze

Kazegumo

Yugumo

Destroyer Squadron 3 (Ijuin)

2306hrs

2249hrs

2304hrs

Chevalier sunk
0311hrs

2245hrs

Destroyer Squadron 4 (Walker)

O'Bannon

Chevalier

Selfridge

2252hrs

2301hrs

2259hrs

2256hrs

2254hrs

2255hrs

Shigure

Samidare

2259hrs

Yugumo

Kazegumo

Isokaze

Akigumo

2256hrs

2303hrs

Yugumo sunk
2310hrs

2317hrs **Akigumo**

Isokaze

Kazegumo

2313hrs

N

Destroyer

0   2 nautical miles

0   2km

ships against the moon. As the Japanese were trying to get the range for a torpedo attack, Walker was tracking the Japanese destroyers on radar. He decided to attack the larger group of four ships located to his southwest on a reciprocal course. The Americans got 14 torpedoes in the water at 2254hrs. One minute later, Walker ordered his three destroyers to open up with their 5in. guns.

Ijuin's clumsy maneuvering had placed his closest ship, *Yugumo*, only 3,300 yards from Walker's lead ship. *Yugumo* became the target of the gunnery from all three American destroyers, and immediately executed a quick turn to launch all eight of her torpedoes at the Americans at 2256hrs. Within minutes, *Yugumo* was struck by at least five shells. She lost steering control and then power and was unable to follow the rest of Ijuin's group which turned to the west to present their sterns to any American torpedoes. *Yugumo* gained revenge when one of her torpedoes struck *Chevalier* and brought her to a stop.

The other two destroyers in Ijuin's force were trailing some five miles behind his main body. These were *Shigure* and *Samidare*, led by the redoubtable Hara. Both ships turned to the northwest at 2259hrs and planned a deliberate torpedo attack on the Americans now steaming on a parallel course. Hara's destroyers put a full salvo of 16 Type 93s in the water. One of these found *Selfridge* at 2306hrs and blew off her bow. Just before the arrival of the Japanese torpedoes, *O'Bannon* had collided with the crippled *Chevalier*.

Walker's entire force was now in total disarray. Ijuin failed to take advantage of this and to finish the Americans off. At 2313hrs, Japanese aircraft spotted the second American destroyer division to the east. Thinking these were the cruisers he had been warned about, Ijuin decided to break off the action. While steaming out of the area, at 2317hrs, he fired a full 24-torpedo salvo at the two American cripples now located some 16,000 yards away, but none hit.

Following the main action, the Japanese small craft reached Vella Lavella and succeeded in picking up all the stranded men waiting to be rescued. This, and the fact they had inflicted more damage, made this a tactical victory for the IJN. Both *Yugumo* and *Chevalier* could not be saved; *Selfridge* returned to service seven months later.

THE AMERICAN INVASION OF BOUGAINVILLE ISLAND

In November, there were a large number of Japanese personnel on Bougainville and its surrounding islands. Of the 40,000 IJA and 20,000 IJN personnel, most were deployed in the southern part of the island. Approximately 5,000 were on the Shortlands, and some 6,000 were at Buka Airfield in the north. The area of Empress Augusta Bay was weakly defended with only 2,000–3,000 troops and the original American plan was to take the Shortlands and possibly establish a beachhead at the Japanese airfield at Kahili. Instead, Halsey decided to employ a leapfrogging strategy again, and bypass the heavily defended areas around the Shortlands and Kahili in favor of a direct landing at Empress Augusta Bay, where he could build his own airfield. In addition to avoiding the teeth of the Japanese defenses, the Cape

Landing craft from the attack transport *American Legion* circle while awaiting landing orders during the invasion of Cape Torokina on November 1, 1943. The invasion beaches are in the background, being shelled, and there are Marine torpedo and dive-bombers over the beaches. On some beaches, there was no Japanese opposition, but the landing encountered a rolling surf which was higher and rougher than expected, which resulted in many wrecked landing craft. (Official Marine Corps photo courtesy of Marine Corps History Division)

Torokina area of Empress Augusta Bay was so remote that Halsey's staff correctly assessed it would take the Japanese months to move enough forces to the area for a large-scale counterattack.

For his landing on Bougainville, Halsey had available a single carrier group comprised of *Saratoga* and light carrier *Princeton*, escorted by two light cruisers and ten destroyers. The primary surface escorts for the invasion were the four Cleveland-class light cruisers of Merrill's Cruiser Division 12. Three destroyer squadrons were assigned for screening duties. Another small carrier group and Cruiser Division 13 arrived on November 7. The invasion force of 14,321 men was embarked on 12 transports. The most critical aspect of the operation was providing land-based air cover to the invasion since the beachhead was only 210 miles from Rabaul. Throughout October, AIRSOLS mounted a concerted effort to neutralize Kahili, Kara, Ballale, Buka, and Bonis with a total of 3,259 sorties.

The Japanese were uncertain of the next American target. Rabaul anticipated a possible landing at Cape Torokina, but local commanders on Bougainville were thinking that the Shortlands was more likely, a perception shaped at least in part by a landing of a predominantly New Zealand force on the Treasury Islands located some 25 miles southwest of the Shortlands on October 27 and a raid on Choiseul Island located to the east of the Shortlands on the same day with the Marine 2nd Parachute Battalion. Accordingly, Japanese ground forces were deployed to meet an attack on southern Bougainville. However, it was clear that an American operation was in the offing, so Koga moved his carrier air groups from Truk down to Rabaul, beginning on October 28. By November 1, a total of 173 carrier aircraft (82 fighters, 45 Vals, 40 Kates, and six reconnaissance aircraft) had relocated to the airfields around Rabaul. These joined the approximately 200 aircraft of the Eleventh Air Fleet, which was under severe pressure from General Kenney's Fifth Army Air Force.

THE LANDING

Beginning on October 28, three groups totaling 12 transports carrying the assault echelons of the 3rd Marine Division departed for Empress Augusta Bay. The transports were lightly loaded to facilitate a quick unloading and departure. This was key since never before had a major amphibious operation been mounted so close to a major Japanese airbase. The transit to the invasion area went smoothly and was unobserved by the Japanese. The first troops hit one of 12 beaches at 0726hrs on November 1; in total, the first wave moved 7,000–8,000 troops ashore. The actual invasion area was covered by only 270 Japanese troops with a single 75mm gun. The small defending force and its well-placed 75mm gun sank four landing craft and damaged ten others, causing 70 Marine casualties. By nightfall, the beachhead was secure and some 14,000 men and 6,200 tons of supplies were safely ashore.

The Japanese air reaction was also ineffective. At 0735hrs, the first attack arrived with 44 fighters escorting nine dive-bombers. The combat air patrol of 16 Allied fighters prevented most of the Japanese aircraft from reaching the beachhead. The only damage was a near-miss inflicted on a US Navy destroyer. The second wave of about 100 IJN carrier aircraft flying from Rabaul arrived at about 1300hrs and met a determined and well-directed defense of 34 Allied fighters. No damage was suffered by any American ship. By 1730hrs, eight of the 12 transports were completely unloaded. With the report of a Japanese surface force departing Rabaul, all 12 transports were ordered to leave the area. The largest naval battle of the Solomons campaign was about to begin.

THE BATTLE OF EMPRESS AUGUSTA BAY

The landings at Empress Augusta Bay prompted the IJN to mount its first major operation in the South Pacific since the conclusion of the Guadalcanal campaign. The well-timed arrival of the heavy cruisers *Myoko* and *Haguro* in Rabaul as part of a convoy escort gave Admiral Samejima enough combat power to challenge the US Navy in a major action. At 1000hrs on October 31, the two heavy cruisers, escorted by two light cruisers and two destroyers, under the command of Vice Admiral Omori Sentaro, were ordered to leave Rabaul to intercept a US Navy task force headed for Buka. This was Merrill's light cruiser force ordered to conduct a pre-invasion bombardment of the airfield there. The Japanese interception was unsuccessful, and Omori returned to Rabaul by 1100hrs on November 1. By this time, word of the American landing at Cape Torokina had reached Rabaul. Samejima ordered Omori to escort five destroyer transports for a counterlanding and then attack the American landing force. Samejima scraped up another four destroyers to add to Omori's force. This scratch force had no chance to go over a battle plan and the results would soon be in evidence.

Omori's augmented force departed Rabaul at 1700hrs. The operation soon ran into problems when the rendezvous with the destroyer transports was delayed until 2030hrs. The entire counterlanding part of the operation was discarded after Omori was detected by a submarine and then by an Allied aircraft. Having lost the element of surprise, Omori asked Samejima to call off the counterlanding. This was approved which sent the five destroyer transports back to Rabaul. Omori increased speed to attack the American landing force believed to be off Empress Augusta Bay. He did not expect to encounter major surface forces, just helpless transports.

The American plan

The Bougainville invasion was protected by Merrill's cruiser division of four Cleveland-class light cruisers. For this operation, he was also assigned two destroyer divisions with a total of eight Fletcher-class destroyers. Merrill had the advantage of receiving contact reports from aircraft shadowing Omori's force. He intended to fight the battle to the west of Empress Augusta Bay and block any Japanese attempt to get near the beachhead. His plan showed the growing confidence of the US Navy in night actions and incorporated many lessons acquired earlier in the campaign at high cost. Merrill planned to exploit the offensive capabilities of his destroyers by letting them attack first before unleashing the 6in. guns aboard his cruisers. The biggest difference was that Merrill intended to keep his cruisers at ranges greater than 19,000 yards since the US Navy was finally beginning to understand the true capabilities of the IJN's Type 93 torpedo. The entire force would conduct continuous course changes to minimize the torpedo threat.

Japanese heavy cruiser *Haguro* shown in a pre-war photo in April 1936. Japanese heavy cruisers were an integral part of the IJN's night combat capabilities and had proven to be formidable opponents at night clashes earlier in the war. At Empress Augusta Bay, the two Japanese heavy cruisers present were unable to contend with a US Navy force which employed maneuvers designed to defeat the Japanese Type 93 torpedo. (Naval History and Heritage Command)

The Naval Battle of Empress Augusta Bay, November 2, 1943

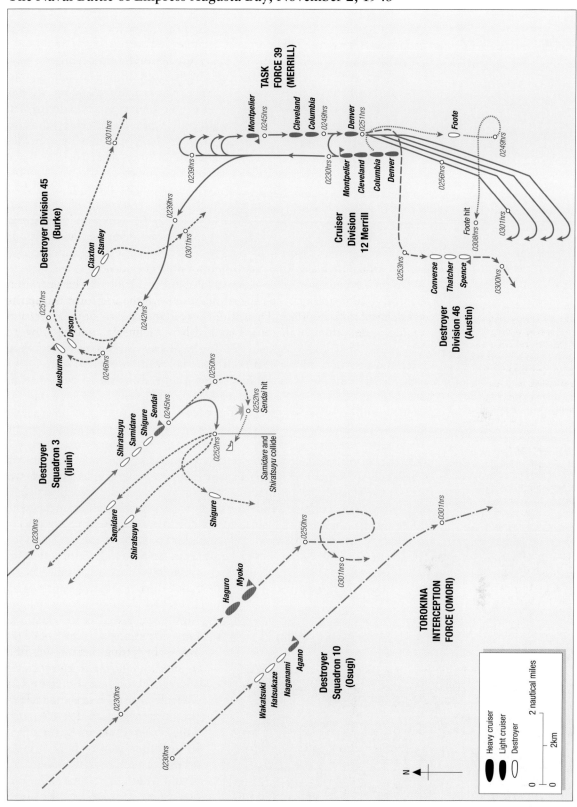

Light cruiser *Denver* photographed entering Havannah Harbor, Efate, New Hebrides, on April 22, 1943. Note the cruiser's Curtiss SOC Seagull floatplane in the right foreground. *Denver* was part of the US Navy force which defeated a force which included heavier and more powerful IJN Myoko-class heavy cruisers at Empress Augusta Bay in November 1943. (Naval History and Heritage Command)

Light cruiser *Sendai* photographed in February 1939. IJN light cruisers were designed to act as flagships for destroyer squadrons, as shown in this photograph, and were not heavily armed or armored. *Sendai* was crippled by 6in. gunfire at Empress Augusta bay. (Naval History and Heritage Command)

The battle opens

The actual battle turned out to be a confused affair for both sides. Omori had received reports of transports unloading in Empress Augusta Bay, so changed course at 0200hrs to head toward them. He arrayed his force in three columns with his two heavy cruisers in the center, and two flanking columns of a light cruiser leading three destroyers. As the Japanese approached, Merrill's force was steaming to the northwest some 20 miles west of the beachhead. At 0227hrs, radar on the cruiser *Montpelier* detected the Japanese 35,900 yards away. This prompted Merrill to change his heading to due north. At 0231hrs, the four destroyers in Burke's division were cut loose to make their torpedo attacks. Minutes later, the cruisers reversed course to the south while the rear division of destroyers were ordered to attack the southernmost Japanese column.

It was not until 0245hrs that Omori received reports that Merrill's force was in the area. This was the result of a Japanese aircraft dropping a flare over the US Navy force which allowed light cruiser *Sendai*, leading the northern column, to spot the Americans. Burke launched 25 torpedoes at the column led by *Sendai* at 0246hrs; between 0250 and 0252hrs, *Samidare* replied with a full salvo of eight torpedoes. At this time, Merrill decided he could no longer wait for the results of Burke's torpedo attack, so he ordered his cruisers to open fire. The primary target was *Sendai* since she was the closest and largest radar return. The cruiser was quickly struck by an unknown number of 6in. shells which hit her boiler rooms and jammed the rudder. The ship lost power. The two destroyers behind *Sendai*, *Samidare* and *Shiratsuyu*, collided while making evasive maneuvers to escape the deluge of 6in. shells. Both headed to the northwest but eventually returned to stand by the stricken *Sendai*. While the initial US Navy gunnery barrage was effective, the initial American torpedo barrage was not. A well-timed turn by Omori meant that all 25 torpedoes missed.

While Merrill maneuvered to keep the range at about 19,000 yards, the Japanese cruisers opened up with their main batteries at Merrill's cruisers. By this time, Merrill's cruisers had shifted fire to the other two Japanese columns. This created more confusion; the column led by light cruiser *Agano* turned to the west and ran across Omori's two heavy cruisers. Destroyer *Hatsukaze*, the third

First destroyer squadron at anchor. Cruiser Sendai flagship.

ship in the column, attempted to move between the two heavy cruisers and collided with *Myoko* at 0307hrs. *Haguro* barely missed hitting the destroyer *Wakatsuki*.

While the Japanese were having problems not running into each other, Merrill's cruisers were deftly executing a series of high-speed maneuvers meant to make the fire-control solutions for Japanese gunners and torpedomen as difficult as possible. He also made sure to keep his distance from the Japanese. When the range closed to 13,000 yards at 0326hrs, he conducted a 180-degree course change to north to open the range once again. However, radical maneuvering by Merrill's cruisers made it difficult to bring accurate fire on Omori's ships. Nevertheless, *Haguro* was hit by six shells, though four of them failed to detonate so damage was minimal. At 0315hrs, the Japanese heavy cruisers opened up again with torpedoes and 8in. guns. Japanese gunnery was accurate, and the US Navy cruisers were quickly straddled with 8in. shells. Between 0320 and 0325hrs, the lead cruiser, *Denver*, took three 8in. hits, but these were also duds. The light cruiser *Columbia* was also hit by a single 8in. shell which failed to explode.

As usual in a night action, both sides made extravagant claims of damage to the other. Omori was confident he had sunk several cruisers. This supposed success had not come cheaply; *Sendai* was crippled by gunfire and three destroyers were victims of collision damage. Thinking he could achieve nothing else, and believing he was facing as many as seven American heavy cruisers, he ordered his force to retire at 0337hrs. The only remaining part of the battle was the actions by the two American destroyer divisions. Burke's division took over an hour to get back into the fray after its opening unsuccessful torpedo barrage. Re-entering the battle, it came across the sinking *Sendai* and engaged her with 5in. gunfire. The retreating *Samidare* and *Shiratsuyu* were detected by radar, but before Burke could engage them, the second destroyer division advised Burke not to open fire to avoid a friendly fire incident. This confusion allowed the two Japanese destroyers to escape. The damaged *Hatsukaze* was not so lucky. She was engaged by both American destroyer divisions and sank at 0539hrs with all hands.

The only significant damage suffered by the US Navy was to the rear destroyer division. The activities of this unit demonstrated the difficulties inherent in coordinating forces in a night engagement. The destroyers were unable to carry out Merrill's battle plan to conduct an opening torpedo attack. After losing contact with the rest of the division, *Foote* was hit by a torpedo meant for Merrill's cruisers and had her stern blown off. The ship came to a stop, and was barely missed by the cruiser *Cleveland* and destroyer *Spence*. Later, the remaining three destroyers had an excellent torpedo set-up against the Japanese heavy cruisers, but did not take the shot because the contacts were thought to be friendly ships. Coming across *Sendai*, they fired eight torpedoes at her at 0328hrs, of which two probably

After Koga learned of the defeat at Empress Augusta Bay, he ordered seven heavy cruisers, one light cruiser, and four destroyers to move to Rabaul from Truk. This was a surface force overwhelmingly more powerful than anything Halsey had in the South Pacific. With the fate of the Bougainville invasion in the balance, Halsey ordered the carriers *Saratoga* and *Princeton* to attack the Japanese force in Simpson Harbor. The carriers launched an all-out strike with 97 aircraft on the morning of November 5, relying on land-based fighters to cover the carriers from Japanese air attack. Four of the heavy cruisers were damaged, ending the threat to the Bougainville beachhead. This photo shows the attack in progress. The cruiser in the left center of the view with the fire aft is *Maya*. Several other cruisers are among the ships heading for sea, to the right. (Naval History and Heritage Command)

RABAUL RAID.

MERRILL'S CRUISERS AT EMPRESS AUGUSTA BAY (PP. 78–79)

The largest naval battle of the entire Solomons campaign was the Battle of Empress Augusta Bay on November 2. In this engagement, a US Navy force led by four Cleveland-class light cruisers out-fought and out-maneuvered an IJN force which included two heavy cruisers. This scene depicts the leading cruisers of Rear Admiral Merrill's Cruiser Division 12 during the peak of the gunnery duel with Japanese heavy cruisers *Haguro* and *Myoko*. The lead ship is Merrill's flagship *Montpelier* (1), followed by *Cleveland* (2). Both ships have their 6in. battery trained to port and are firing furiously at the Japanese (3). During the battle, the four American light cruisers fired 4,591 6in. rounds; despite the fact that the Americans were using radar fire control, only a handful of hits were scored and several of these were duds. Japanese gunnery did not use radar, but was still accurate as the straddles around *Montpelier* indicate (4). However, none of the shells hit *Montpelier* and damage from 8in. shells to Merrill's other cruisers was minor.

hit. At 0352hrs, 19 more torpedoes were fired at the retreating *Samidare* and *Shiratsuyu* with no result. At 0425hrs, Burke's destroyers engaged them with gunfire to no effect.

As morning dawned, Merrill recalled his destroyers and prepared to repel a likely Japanese air attack at daylight. Just before 0800hrs, a formation of 80 Zero fighters escorting 18 Val dive-bombers flew over the damaged *Foote* and attacked the cruisers steaming in a circular anti-aircraft formation. Allied fighters providing combat air patrol claimed eight Japanese aircraft, and only two hits were recorded, both on *Montpelier*'s stern, which inflicted minor damage.

Marine M3 light tanks supporting an attack on Bougainville. Tanks were used to crush the Japanese counterlanding on November 8, but subsequently played little role in the campaign because of the hilly terrain inland from the beachhead. (Official Marine Corps photo courtesy of Marine Corps History Division)

The battle ended in a significant victory for the US Navy. For the cost of torpedo damage to a destroyer and some light shell damage to two cruisers and two destroyers, the Americans had shattered the only real Japanese attempt to attack the Bougainville landings. In the process, they had sunk a light cruiser and a destroyer, and damaged two heavy cruisers and two destroyers. Merrill's handling of the battle was outstanding since his constant maneuvering had negated the IJN's most powerful weapon, the Type 93 torpedo. His battle plan was good, though the destroyer divisions failed to perform as expected. As usual in a night engagement, radar-guided gunfire seemed impressive, but proved inaccurate. Of the 4,591 6in. shells fired, less then 20 hit. However, these were sufficient to cripple *Sendai* and shatter the Japanese formation. The performance of Omori's scratch formation was weak in all areas. Basic maneuvering proved to be a real problem, accounting for the eventual loss of a destroyer. The Japanese destroyers were not handled aggressively, and Japanese gunfire proved even more inaccurate than the US Navy's. As a result, Omori was relieved of command and the SLOCs to the beachhead were never threatened again by surface attack.

EXPANSION OF THE BOUGAINVILLE BEACHHEAD

The landing at Cape Torokina had gone according to plan with little interruption from the Japanese. The 3rd Marine Division was firmly ashore, and the 37th Division, located in Guadalcanal, would arrive soon to expand the beachhead. The Japanese were slow to respond since they believed the Cape Torokina operation was a diversion. They still expected the main American attack against the airfields located on southern or northern Bougainville. Nevertheless, in typical IJA fashion, Imamura decided to send a totally inadequate force to the Cape Torokina area to mop up the American beachhead. The initial reaction force consisted of two battalions from the 23rd Infantry Regiment from the area of Buin in southern Bougainville. In support, a counterlanding operation against the American beachhead was planned using elements from the 17th Infantry Division in Rabaul.

Japanese doctrine called for a quick-response counterlanding against an American beachhead before the invaders could firmly establish themselves. And on November 7, the Japanese actually executed a counterlanding for one of the few times in the war. The force assigned to conduct the operation was specially trained for this type of operation, but at approximately 475 men it was totally inadequate for its mission. The Japanese did not even have a firm idea where the American beachhead was, but the operation went ahead anyway. From 0400 to 0600hrs on November 7, the small force went ashore from four destroyer transports north of the American beachhead. After the scattered Japanese collected themselves, they launched an attack on the Marine perimeter but made no headway against two Marine battalions. By the afternoon, and into the next day, the Japanese were virtually annihilated by an attack supported by an intensive artillery preparation and light tanks. The ill-conceived and unsupported Japanese counterlanding operation had ended in total failure.

The Marines proceeded to advance inland to gain control of trails which channeled all movement through the rainforest. Against the two battalions of the 23rd Infantry Regiment, Geiger sent the three battalions of the 1st Parachute Regiment, the 2nd Raider Regiment, and the 9th and 31st Marines. With the help of artillery, the Marines pushed the Japanese 5,000 yards from the beach by November 14 which provided enough space for the three naval construction battalions landed on D-Day to begin work on the two main airfields located near the Piva River. Meanwhile, the 37th Infantry Division took over the left flank of the beachhead, but saw almost no action. By November 21, the beachhead was firmly established with two complete divisions ashore along with corps troops and construction units. The beachhead was comprised of 16,000 yards of perimeter, including 7,000 along the beach.

A further expansion of the beachhead was undertaken in response to the Japanese using the high ground northeast of the beachhead to shell the airfields. On December 18, the Marines seized Hellzapoppin Ridge which had been tenaciously defended by the Japanese using positions on its reverse slope to escape air and artillery bombardment. After 12 days of incessant Marine

DIRECT HIT ON JAP MACHINE GUN NEST

attacks, supported by artillery and air attacks, the ridge finally fell. The most important factor in its capture, according to the Marines, was one of the first instances of close air support in the Pacific War. Guided by a ground controller with a radio from a damaged Marine aircraft, Marine dive-bombers were able to deliver their ordnance within 75 yards of the Marines on the ridge. The nearby Hill 600A was seized by the 21st Marines on December 24. With this, the final shape of the Cape Torokina perimeter was established and major fighting brought to an end.

In its final configuration, the inland part of the American perimeter stretched 22,500 yards. Work on defensive entrenchments began on November 25 and were complete in some areas by December 15. The defenses were formidable with pre-sited primary and secondary positions for all weapons, fields of fire cleared out to 100 yards, twin rows of barbed wire, and searchlights for night illumination.

The first large Marine elements to leave Bougainville departed on December 25, 1943. The Marines returned to Guadalcanal to prepare for future battles. The 3rd Marine Division went on to fight on Guam in July–August 1944 and Iwo Jima from February–March 1945. (Official Marine Corps photo courtesy of Marine Corps History Division)

Most importantly for the prosecution of future operations against Rabaul, the first airfield inside the perimeter, built along the beach at Cape Torokina, was operational by December 9. Two more airfields were built inland near the Piva River. Piva Uncle, was begun on November 29 and completed on December 30, and Piva Yoko was completed on January 9, 1944.

THE BATTLE OF CAPE ST. GEORGE

The Japanese continued to reinforce Buka since they still believed an American landing was likely there. The last naval battle of the Solomons campaign occurred on November 25 during the final Japanese attempt to move reinforcements to Bougainville by destroyer. For this operation it was planned to load the reinforcements on three destroyers and then evacuate unemployed aviation personnel on the return trip. Escorting the transports were two other destroyers. The entire force was under the command of Captain Kagawa Kiyoto. The first part of the operation went well when the three transport destroyers arrived at Buka late on November 24, quickly loaded their return passengers, and departed at 0045hrs on the 25th.

The Americans knew about the operation beforehand, and five destroyers were dispatched under Commander Burke to effect an interception. When the Japanese departed Buka, Burke's destroyers were waiting. American radar gave Burke the priceless advantage of first detection, and Burke knew what to do with it. After the initial radar contact was gained at 22,000 yards, Burke turned to the east to close the Japanese. When the oblivious Japanese were only 5,500 yards away, he ordered each of his destroyers to fire five torpedoes and immediately made a turn to the south to avoid the expected Japanese counterattack.

Lookouts on the Japanese flagship *Onami* finally spotted the retiring Americans, but it was too late. American torpedoes shredded Kagawa's force. Several torpedoes hit *Onami* which sank with no survivors. The second destroyer in the column, *Makinami*, was hit by a single torpedo, but the ship

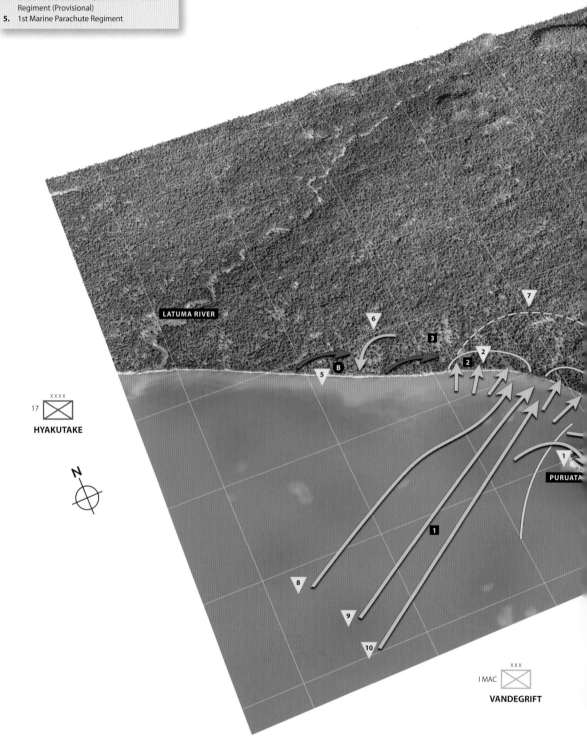

AMERICAN FORCES
1. 3rd Marine Division assault echelon (3rd and 9th Marines, 2nd and 3rd Raider Battalions, 3rd Defense Battalion, 12th Marines)
2. 3rd Battalion, 9th Marines
3. 1st Battalion, 21st Marines
4. 2nd and 3rd Battalions, 2nd Marine Raider Regiment (Provisional)
5. 1st Marine Parachute Regiment

LATUMA RIVER

17 ✕✕✕✕ ⊠
HYAKUTAKE

N

PURUATA

I MAC ✕✕✕ ⊠
VANDEGRIFT

THE INVASION OF BOUGAINVILLE, NOVEMBER 1, 1943
The Americans expand their beachhead

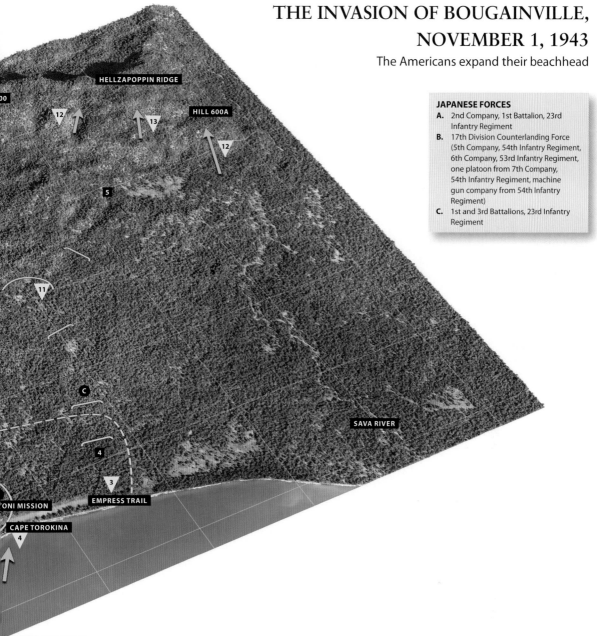

JAPANESE FORCES

A. 2nd Company, 1st Battalion, 23rd Infantry Regiment

B. 17th Division Counterlanding Force (5th Company, 54th Infantry Regiment, 6th Company, 53rd Infantry Regiment, one platoon from 7th Company, 54th Infantry Regiment, machine gun company from 54th Infantry Regiment)

C. 1st and 3rd Battalions, 23rd Infantry Regiment

HELLZAPOPPIN RIDGE

HILL 600A

SAVA RIVER

EMPRESS TRAIL

ONI MISSION

CAPE TOROKINA

▼ EVENTS

1. November 1: in brief heavy fighting, the dug-in Japanese defenders at Cape Torokina are destroyed by the 3rd Marine Regiment by 1100hrs. The 9th Marines, landing on the left, see no action. The 3rd Raider Battalion takes Puruata Island directly off shore.

2. By the end of D-Day, the 3rd Marine Division holds a shallow beachhead some 3 miles wide.

3. November 5: fighting begins inland between the Japanese 23rd Infantry Regiment and elements of the 9th and 21st Marines for control of key trails.

4. November 6: the 21st Marine Regiment arrives.

5. 0400–0600hrs, November 7: 475 men from the Japanese 17th Division conduct a counterlanding north of the beachhead in 21 landing craft. Local fighting results in small gains for the Japanese against 3rd Battalion, 9th Marines.

6. November 7: 1st Battalion, 21st Marines, following a heavy artillery barrage and supported by light tanks, annihilates the Japanese force.

7. By November 7, against sporadic resistance and in difficult terrain, the beachhead is expanded to a depth of 2,000 yards inland.

8. November 8: the 148th RCT of the 37th Division arrives and assumes positions on the left flank of the beachhead.

9. November 13: the 129th RCT arrives.

10. November 19: the 145th RCT arrives.

11. November 20: Geiger begins to expand his beachhead. The 37th Division meets no opposition, but the 3rd Marine Division meets resistance from elements of the 23rd Infantry Regiment.

12. December 9–27: shelling of the airfields from the high ground northeast of the beachhead prompts Geiger to expand the beachhead further. The advance is conducted by the 9th and 21st Marines, assisted by the 1st Marine Parachute Regiment.

13. December 25: the 21st Marine Regiment captures Hellzapoppin Ridge.

Uzuki, shown here in the late 1920s, was a Mutsuki-class destroyer launched in 1925. Assigned to the transport group at the Battle of Cape St. George, she survived the battle with minor damage. (Naval History and Heritage Command)

remained afloat. With the Japanese covering force out of action, the Americans gained contact on the Japanese transport group some 13,000 yards to the northeast. Burke took off in pursuit and a classic tail chase ensued. The American destroyers strained at 33 knots to overtake the fleeing Japanese while engaging the Japanese with their two forward 5in. mounts. *Yugiri* turned briefly to fire three torpedoes at the Americans, but Burke foresaw this and executed a well-timed evasion maneuver. The torpedoes exploded in the wake of Burke's flagship.

At 0225hrs, the three Japanese destroyers split up with each headed on a different course. Burke decided to go after the largest radar contact which turned out to be *Yugiri*. By 0256hrs, the range had closed to 8,800 yards as the Japanese destroyer lost speed as the result of 5in. shell hits. The end game came at 0305hrs when a hit on *Yugiri*'s machinery spaces resulted in an additional loss of speed. Her captain chose to fight and came about to fire his remaining torpedoes and engage with guns. *Yugiri* was overwhelmed by the combined gun and torpedo attacks from Burke's ships and sank at 0328hrs only 60 miles east of Cape George on the island of New Ireland. The last two IJN destroyers reached Rabaul, but the crippled *Makinami* was finished off with torpedoes and guns. Burke's brilliant victory demonstrated that the IJN had lost any advantage it once held in night combat. Three Japanese destroyers were sunk with heavy loss of life, for no American losses.

THE JAPANESE COUNTERATTACK ON BOUGAINVILLE

The 3rd Marine Division had executed its mission of seizing a beachhead on Bougainville with relatively low losses. A total of 423 Marines were killed and 1,418 wounded during the campaign in exchange for estimated Japanese casualties of almost 2,500 killed. The Marines began to depart Bougainville in late December, eventually turning their positions over to the Americal Division.

By February 1944, Rabaul had been essentially neutralized. Japanese ships had stopped using its harbor and the flow of air reinforcements had been stopped. The last interception of an Allied air attack was mounted on February 19. Rabaul was now an afterthought in a war which had passed it by. The garrison of almost 98,000 Japanese were forced to fend for themselves since no further supplies were forthcoming.

A similar situation existed on Bougainville, where significant numbers of Japanese remained on the island. 17th Army planners had finally concluded the obvious and had determined that the Cape Torokina landing was the main American effort on Bougainville. General Hyakutake ordered that the beachhead be attacked. Given the low intelligence estimates that the American force inside the perimeter numbered some 30,000, of which 10,000 were aviation support personnel, there seemed reason for optimism. By bringing the 6th Division and most of the 17th Division against the perimeter, a force totaling 15,000–19,000 men, Hyakutake was confident of success. In actuality, the number of the American combat troops totaled

The Naval Battle of Cape St. George, November 25, 1943

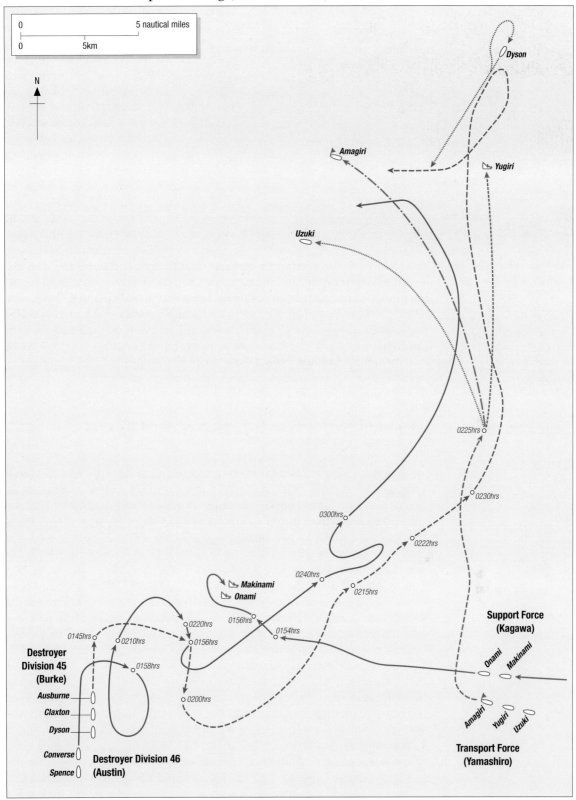

Seabees from Naval Construction Battalion No. 36 look on as the first plane, a Marine Dauntless, lands on Piva Airfield on Bougainville on December 19, 1943. The airfields on Bougainville played a key role in tightening the stranglehold around Rabaul. (Naval History and Heritage Command)

about 27,000 men and total personnel in the perimeter were 62,000. Not only were the Japanese outnumbered, but they were attacking an entrenched defender well supplied with artillery and air support. The Japanese could bring comparatively little firepower to bear. The entire operation was hopeless and owed its existence to the stubbornness and pride of the IJA.

True to the estimates of Halsey's staff in October 1943, it took the Japanese several months to move a large force to attack the beachhead. From the south, the 6th Infantry Division moved up both coasts while the 17th Infantry Division moved toward the perimeter from the north. The Americans were able to trace these movements easily using a variety of sources. More importantly, Hyakutake's battle plan was taken from dead Japanese allowing the Americans to make precise preparations for the attack.

The attack plan was built around three assault groups, each named after its commander. The Japanese plan was needlessly complicated, and failed to mass its limited force in a single attack to overwhelm a small segment in the American line. Had this been done, the Japanese might have been able to break into the American rear areas and cause massive chaos and destruction. The Iwasa Unit would open the attack on March 8 from the north and penetrate to the Piva River Airfields. The Muda Unit would widen the breach on March 12. Finally, the Magata Unit would attack from the east on March 11 and join the attack on the airfields. All three units would then drive south to complete the destruction of the American beachhead by March 17. The 17th Infantry Division group was to act as a reserve or conduct diversionary attacks on the northwest section of the perimeter.

The American defense

The defense of the perimeter was assigned to XIV Corps under Major-General Griswold. As described earlier, American defensive positions were strong and Griswold also possessed the advantage of interior lines. Twelve infantry battalions were placed in the front lines with another six in reserve. Each battalion held a frontage of between 2,000 and 2,400 yards. The 37th Infantry Division maintained its positions on the left, with the Americal Division replacing the Marines on the right. Available artillery consisted of the eight battalions (two 155mm and six 105mm) from the two divisions, and two 155mm gun batteries from the 3rd Marine Defense Battalion.

The Japanese attack

When Japanese artillery began to pound the Piva Airfields on the morning of March 8, it was obvious the final Japanese bid for victory on Bougainville was underway. The following day, as planned, the Iwasa Unit kicked off the offensive. The lead 23rd Infantry Regiment attacked a sector held by the 145th Infantry Regiment in a night assault and created a salient in the American lines in the area of Hill 700. Later in the day, the 145th Infantry Regiment's reserve battalion attacked the salient and restored most of the original line. Early on March 10, the Japanese resumed their attack but were pulverized by American firepower. American counterattacks later in the day, supported by engineers, made further progress in reducing the salient. Fierce combat continued into the night when the Japanese made mass attacks in the same sector in a final attempt to break through. The attack was stopped again in the face of heavy American artillery fire.

For the next two days, the Americans steadily ground down the Japanese salient around Hill 700. Another reserve infantry battalion was committed on March 11, but made limited progress. Finally on March 12, the Iwasa Unit was forced to give up its slender gains and withdrew. In the course of four days of bitter fighting, American firepower proved decisive. During that period, 20,802 105mm, about 10,000 75mm, and almost 14,000 mortar rounds were used to pulverize the Japanese.

The Muda Unit attacked on March 10 and was quickly hung up on Hill 260 where the Americans had established an observation post manned by 260 men. Griswold ordered the commander of the 37th Infantry Division to hold the post at all costs, even though it was in an exposed position one-half mile from the main defensive perimeter. After three days of continued bombardment and attacks, the Japanese still held the South Knob of the hill. Griswold denied requests to withdraw from the hill, so combat continued for another several days until the Japanese withdrew and the South Knob was occupied on March 18. During the action, 10,000 105mm shells were used against the Japanese defenders.

The third prong of the Japanese offensive also foundered under the weight of American firepower. On March 11, the Magata Unit attacked with two battalions over fairly flat terrain against the well-dug-in and waiting 2nd Battalion, 129th Infantry Regiment. The attack came in at dusk and made two minor penetrations. In what came to be a pattern, the next day American reserves regained most of the former line. On March 13, the Americans committed tanks to the counterattack. The attacks were repeated on March 15 and 17.

With none of their attacks making any serious headway, Hyakutake and Kanda decided to mass all their remaining forces for a last attack on March 23. After regrouping from the areas around Hill 700 and 260, all remaining Japanese units again attacked the sector manned by the American 129th Infantry Regiment. The attack began after dark, but the Americans knew where and when it was coming, so were able to mass fires on the assault and break it up before it got going. The next day, minor penetrations were cleaned up by counterattacks supported by seven artillery battalions and a heavy mortar battalion.

The final Japanese attacks on Bougainville ended in total defeat. The Japanese lost over 5,000 dead and had another 3,000 wounded. American dead totaled 263. XIV Corps conducted a pursuit of the defeated Japanese until April 13–14 to push the Japanese out of artillery range of the Piva airfields. By the end of April, they reported capturing four 105mm howitzers, one 105 mm gun, and 28 75mm artillery pieces. The offensive power of the 17th Army was broken for the remainder of the war.

17 XXXX HYAKUTAKE

PIVA YOKE

LATUMA RIVER

N

PURUATA ISLAN

XIV XXX GRISWOLD

THE JAPANESE COUNTERATTACK, MARCH 1944

American firepower proves decisive

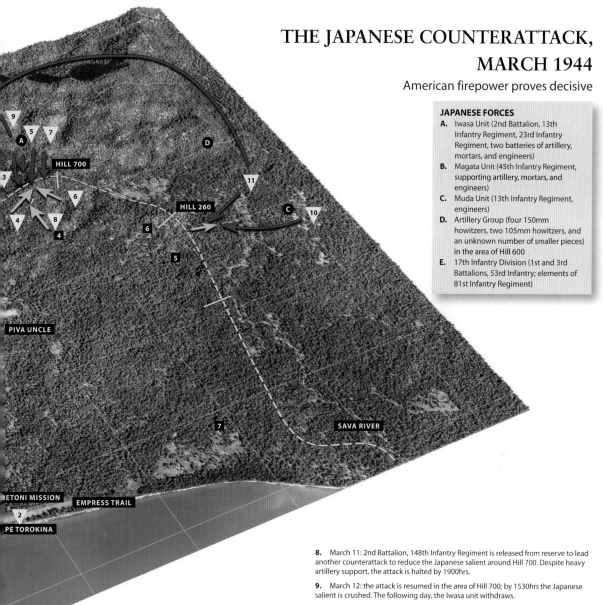

JAPANESE FORCES

A. Iwasa Unit (2nd Battalion, 13th Infantry Regiment, 23rd Infantry Regiment, two batteries of artillery, mortars, and engineers)

B. Magata Unit (45th Infantry Regiment, supporting artillery, mortars, and engineers)

C. Muda Unit (13th Infantry Regiment, engineers)

D. Artillery Group (four 150mm howitzers, two 105mm howitzers, and an unknown number of smaller pieces) in the area of Hill 600

E. 17th Infantry Division (1st and 3rd Battalions, 53rd Infantry; elements of 81st Infantry Regiment)

▼ EVENTS

1. 0545hrs, March 8: Japanese artillery targets the Piva airfields destroying four aircraft and damaging 19; all but six aircraft are moved to New Georgia.

2. March 9: Japanese guns force the evacuation of aircraft from the Cape Torokina fighter strip.

3. March 9: attacks by the Iwasa's Unit 23rd Infantry Regiment against the 145th Infantry Regiment begin after midnight and create a salient in the American lines in the area of Hill 700.

4. March 9: 1st Battalion, 145th Infantry Regiment, released from reserve and, supported by tanks, restores most of the American line.

5. 0645hrs, March 10: the 23rd Infantry Regiment resumes its attack, but makes no progress in the face of heavy American artillery and mortar fire.

6. Afternoon, March 10: 1st and 2nd Battalions, 145th Infantry Regiment, supported by engineers, reduce the Japanese penetration by half in heavy fighting.

7. Night, March 10: the Iwasa Unit conducts massed attacks on the 145th Infantry Regiment, but is easily and bloodily repulsed.

8. March 11: 2nd Battalion, 148th Infantry Regiment is released from reserve to lead another counterattack to reduce the Japanese salient around Hill 700. Despite heavy artillery support, the attack is halted by 1900hrs.

9. March 12: the attack is resumed in the area of Hill 700; by 1530hrs the Japanese salient is crushed. The following day, the Iwasa unit withdraws.

10. March 10: the Muda Unit attacks an American observation post on Hill 260 manned by 260 men. The Japanese gain the South Knob of the hill, but are unable to take the North Knob. Ordered to hold the hill, the 182nd Infantry Regiment sends out two companies from its reserve battalion (2nd), but both are repulsed. The next day, the attack reaches the observation post.

11. March 12: the Japanese still hold the South Knob of Hill 260. Fierce combat continues until March 15 when the Japanese decide to withdraw all but a screening force. The entire hill is cleared on March 18.

12. March 11: the Magata Unit attacks the 2nd Battalion, 129th Infantry Regiment at dusk. Two minor penetrations are made. The next day, American reserves regain most of the lost line, and repulse Japanese counterattacks.

13. 0400hrs, March 13: 1st and 3rd Battalions of the 45th Infantry Regiment attack again. The Americans counterattack with tanks from the 754th Tank Battalion and regain almost all of the original line by 1930hrs.

14. March 15: 2nd Battalion, 81st Infantry Regiment reinforces the Japanese attack and makes minor gains which are erased by an American counterattack led by tanks. The same thing is repeated on March 17.

15. March 23: after regrouping from the areas around Hill 700 and 260, the Japanese concentrate all their remaining forces on a final attack against the 129th Infantry Regiment. The attack starts after dark, but the Americans know it is coming so use artillery and mortars to break it up before it can gain any momentum. The next day, minor penetrations are cleaned up by counterattacks supported by seven artillery battalions and a heavy mortar battalion.

THE AFTERMATH

THE END ON BOUGAINVILLE

The March 1944 Japanese offensive against the American enclave on Bougainville was not the end to the bloody fighting on the island. XIV Corps remained on the island until the end of the year, when it was relieved to take part in the invasion of the Philippines. During that time, the Americans decided to leave the remaining Japanese on the island alone since they constituted little threat to the perimeter. In fact, the Japanese garrison was in a perilous state since it was forced to grow its own food to survive and, shockingly for the IJA, recorded open instances of insubordination and desertion.

The Americans were replaced by the Australian II Corps comprised of the 3rd Division and the 11th and 23rd Brigades. While the Americans had been content to defend the airfields and let the Japanese garrison wither away, the commander of the Australian Army, General Sir Thomas Blamey had different ideas. He wanted to destroy the Japanese wherever they were, even if they were no more than starving soldiers on a bypassed island. The Australians began their offensive to clear the island in late December, concentrating on southern Bougainville where the majority of the Japanese remained. The Australians advanced relentlessly and efficiently, crushing a Japanese counterattack on April 5 with the loss of approximately 1,620 of the 2,400 Japanese troops involved. After this, Kanda adopted a tactic of harassing the advancing Australians instead of mounting a concerted defense. The Australian offensive continued until June when it was brought to a halt by incessant rains. The six months of fighting resulted in 516 Australian dead and another 1,572 wounded. The bloodletting for the Japanese was extreme. The total Japanese garrison on November 1, 1943 at the start of the battle numbered some 60,000 IJA and IJN personnel. When the Japanese surrendered on September 8, 1945, only 14,546 IJA and 9,366 IJN men remained to be counted by the Australians.

THE SOLOMONS CAMPAIGN—AN ASSESSMENT

The outcome of the battle for New Georgia was never in doubt, but it took much longer and was much more costly than the Americans had planned. Overall, the operation was poorly planned and executed. When one division had proved unable to seize the island, elements of three had to be committed. The battle for a single island, essentially for an advance of five miles to the airfield, had taken some five weeks. American combat casualties were not extremely high (1,187 dead and missing and 4,407 wounded), but sick and combat fatigue casualties were. The 25th and 43rd Divisions took months to recover.

Halsey avoided a similar slugfest by bypassing heavily defended Kolombangara in favor of undefended Vella Lavella. This proved the viability of the Allied island-hopping strategy, though the victory was tainted by the escape of the large Japanese garrison on Kolombangara. The campaign in the central Solomons was ultimately successful since four airfields were seized or built to cover the invasion of Bougainville. The 350 aircraft based on these fields made the landing at Cape Torokina possible.

Bougainville was another example of the Americans successfully executing their bypass strategy. It demonstrated the folly of the Japanese defensive strategy since the IJA could never cover all possible landing areas, especially on the perimeter of Japan's defenses where many potential alternatives existed for the Americans to target. The Japanese counterattack in March 1944 had no prospect of success and was an anticlimactic end to combat on the island between the IJA and the Americans.

The advance up the Solomons was planned to be a prelude to the capture of Rabaul. The slow pace of this advance against what were relatively minor Japanese forces gave the Americans pause. By June 1943, American planners began to realize that considerable time and forces could be spared if Rabaul was isolated and not captured. The offensive in the Central Pacific could not be mounted without taking forces from the South Pacific. Both the US Army and Navy were behind the push to modify the plan to capture Rabaul. By August, at the Quebec Conference, the Joint Chiefs recommended that Rabaul be isolated, not captured. This meant that the large Japanese force on New Britain survived until September 4 when 57,225 IJA and 31,923 IJN personnel surrendered.

From a strategic perspective, the Solomons campaign was probably not the best investment of American resources. It took the Americans from February until December to advance the roughly 400nm from Guadalcanal to Bougainville. To do so required five Army and Marine divisions and large naval and air forces. In comparison, the Japanese economy-of-force operations to delay in the Solomons looked like a wise investment. For the Americans it was a rough start on the Road to Japan, but the lessons learned in the Solomons assisted the Americans in 1944 when the pace of operations dramatically increased.

BIBLIOGRAPHY

Altobello, Brian, *Into the Shadows Furious*, Presidio, Novato, California (2000)

Chapin, John C., *Top of the Ladder: Marine Operations in the Northern Solomons*, Marine Corps Historical Center, Washington, DC (1997)

Craven Wesley F. and Cate, James L., ed., *The Army Air Forces in World War II. Volume Four, The Pacific: Guadalcanal to Saipan August 1942 To July 1944*, Office of Air Force History, Washington, DC (1983)

Day, Ronnie, *New Georgia*, Indiana University Press, Bloomington, Indiana (2016)

Fuquea, David C., *Bougainville*, Naval War College Review, Winter 1997

Gailey, Harry A., *Bougainville 1943–1945*, The University Press of Kentucky, Lexington (1991)

Hammel, Eric, *Munda Trail*, Orion Books, New York (1989)

Horton, D. C., *New Georgia pattern for victory*, Ballantine Books, New York (1971)

Japanese Monograph No. 35, *Southeast Area Operations Record, Volume II, February 1943–August 1945*

Japanese Monograph No. 99, *Southeast Area Naval Operations Record, Part II, February–October 1943*

Japanese Monograph No. 100, *Southeast Area Naval Operations Record, Part III, October 1943–February 1944*

Koburger, Charles W., Jr., *Pacific Turning Point*, Praeger, Westport, Connecticut (1995)

McGee, William L., *The Solomons Campaigns*, BMC Publications, Santa Barbara, California (2002)

Miller, John, *Cartwheel: The Reduction of Rabaul, The United States Army in World War II*, Department of the Army, Washington, DC (1959)

Morison, Samuel E., *Breaking the Bismarcks Barrier, Vol VI History of United States Naval Operations in World War II*, Little, Brown and Company, Boston (1975)

Newell, Reg, *The Battle for Vella Lavella*, McFarland & Company, Inc., Publishers, Jefferson, North Carolina (2016)

O'Hara, Vincent P., *The US Navy Against the Axis*, Naval Institute Press, Annapolis, Maryland (2007)

Prados, John, *Islands of Destiny*, NAL Caliber, New York (2012)

Rentz, John, *Bougainville and the Northern Solomons*, Headquarters US Marine Corps, Washington, DC (1948)

Shaw, Henry I., and Kane, Douglas T., *History of US Marine Corps Operations in World War II, Volume II, Isolation of Rabaul*, Historical Branch, G-3 Division, Headquarters, US Marine Corps (1963)

INDEX

Page numbers in **bold** refer to illustrations and their captions.